WHAT ARE THEY SAYING ABOUT
THE PARABLES?

What Are They Saying About the Parables?

David B. Gowler

PAULIST PRESS
New York/Mahwah, N.J.

Cover design by James Brisson

Library of Congress Cataloging-in-Publication Data

Gowler, David B., 1958-
    What are they saying about the parables? / David B. Gowler.
        p.   cm.
    Includes bibliographical references and index.
    ISBN 0-8091-3962-6 (alk. paper)
    1. Jesus Christ—Parables. I. Title.
BT375.2.G69 2000
226.8′06—dc21

                                                                00-027346

Published by Paulist Press
997 Macarthur Boulevard
Mahwah, New Jersey 07430

www.paulistpress.com

Printed and bound in the
United States of America

Contents

Introduction   1

1. Historical-Critical Approaches to the Parables   3

2. The Emergence of Literary Approaches to the Parables   16

3. Fully Developed Literary Approaches to the Parables   28

4. The Parables and Their Jewish Contexts   41

5. The Parables and Their Hellenistic Contexts   57

6. The Parables and Their Social Contexts   68

7. From Simile and Metaphor to Symbol
   and Emblematic Language   85

Conclusion   102

Notes   104

For Further Reading   139

Scripture Index   148

For my mother and father,

Betty L. Gowler
and
Cedric M. Gowler, Sr.

Introduction

If studied correctly, "the parables will receive a like interpretation from all." So wrote Irenaeus, the second-century Christian theologian, in his work *Against Heresies* (Book 2, Chapter XXVII). His own writings concerning the parables, however, as well as the eighteen intervening centuries challenge that assessment. He and other early church theologians, such as Tertullian, Clement of Alexandria, Origen, and Augustine, all relied on the extensive use of allegory to explain (more "fully") the simple narratives in the gospels we call parables.[1] The radical divergences and complexity of various interpretations in recent studies on the parables only serve to reinforce the point that these short narratives continue to challenge our minds, hearts, and imaginations.

This book will introduce as succinctly as possible the energetic scholarly discussions about the parables of Jesus. I will set the discussions in context and highlight contemporary problems, debates, and current avenues of study. Because of the nature of my task and goals for this series, the discussions must be representative, not exhaustive. The objective is not breadth of knowledge, but depth of insight, and no book can take the place of a careful, informed reading of the parables themselves, for, after all, the caveat noted in rabbinic literature still perfectly evokes the power of parables: "So the parable should not be lightly esteemed in your eyes, since by means of the parable a man arrives at the true meaning of the words of the Torah" (Midrash Song of Songs Rabbah I.1,8).

So to label, as I did above, the parables of Jesus as "simple narratives" is perhaps inaccurate. The complexities of modern scholarship on the parables reflect the parables' own innate and somewhat incongruous complexity—and enigmatic nature. Any book about the parables therefore faces another difficulty. As Richard Pevear notes in his introduction to Fyodor Dostoevsky's *Crime and Punishment,*[2] "the first perplexity of criticism is that it must speak monosemantically of the polysemous" (viii). What is true for Dostoevsky's writings is also true for the polyvalent parables of Jesus: "[T]hey leap out of their historical situation and confront us as if they had not yet spoken their final word" (viii). Appropriately, no final word will be offered here—only a rejoinder within the current dialogues.

I wish to express my appreciation to my own partners in dialogue. Special thanks go to Vernon Robbins, Douglas Low, Doug Chismar, Carol Taylor, Jim Lambeth, and Nancy Gowler Johnson for their critiques of the manuscript. Lawrence Boadt of Paulist Press was exceptionally patient even while I changed—midstream in the writing of this book—to a new position where I was, as he so aptly put it, "busy writing memos." With love and gratitude, I thank my wife Rita and our sons Camden and Jacob. We began this book together during a delightful summer at Yale University, and now we continue on to the next chapter of our lives together. Finally, this book is dedicated to my parents, Cedric and Betty Gowler, who dedicated so much of their lives to their children. To you we owe a debt we cannot repay.

1
Historical-Critical Approaches to the Parables

Modern research on the parables essentially began with Adolph Jülicher's first edition of *Die Gleichnisreden Jesu* in 1886,[1] and—although his categories have been superseded—many of his discussions still influence current debates. For example, Jülicher argues that one must distinguish between the parables of the historical Jesus and the parables as they are found in the Synoptic Gospels (Mt, Mk, Lk). Not only were the parables told thirty to fifty years before the gospels were written down, but the gospel authors themselves were creative expositors of the traditions. For Jülicher, the major problem is that the gospel authors obscured the parabolic message of Jesus with an overgrowth of allegory, descriptive supplementation, and interpretive application. In addition, in a survey of previous interpretations of the parables, Jülicher demonstrates that, with a few exceptions such as John Calvin and John Maldonatus, virtually all interpreters imposed allegorical interpretations far exceeding those found in the gospels themselves.

Jülicher sets out to prune that allegorical overgrowth. Such an approach, of course, not only assumes that an allegorical overgrowth exists, but also that with a proper set of shears and a trained eye, we can pare back the allegorical overgrowth in the gospels to uncover the pristine parables of Jesus. For Jülicher, these properly trimmed, "original" parables demonstrate that Jesus used parables to "illustrate the unfamiliar by the commonly familiar, to guide gently upwards from the easy to the difficult" (I.146).

This understanding of the parables is intimately connected to Jülicher's conception of (a) the form and nature of parables and (b) the meanings intended by the parables. Depending primarily on the work of Aristotle, Jülicher believes that parables are *similes* (comparisons) not metaphors. A metaphor is enigmatic *indirect speech* that says one thing but means another. It remains incomprehensible without interpretation and the proper context. Here Jülicher borrows Aristotle's famous example: "A lion rushed on" could be a metaphor for "Achilles rushed on" (I.52). A simile, on the other hand, is *direct speech,* which is simple, clear, and self-explanatory: "Achilles rushed on like a lion." The simile's purpose is to teach (I.52–58).

The metaphor easily extends into the allegory, which, according to Jülicher, Jesus never used. Instead, Jesus utilized the simile, which can extend into three forms:

1. *Similitude (Gleichnis)*—The similitude contains a commonly recognized occurrence from daily life that is composed of two aspects—the "picture" created by the story and the "object" (or "reality") contained in it. There is one picture and one object/reality portrayed, and the details of the similitude merely provide a colorful background. The interpreter's task is to discover the single point of comparison (the *tertium comparationis*) at which the two parts connect (with a *like* or *as*). This point of comparison challenges the hearer/reader with the necessity of either forming a judgment or making a decision (I.58–80). The saying about the children playing in the marketplace is a similitude (Mt 11:16–19; Lk 7:31–34).

2. *Parable (Parabel)*—The parable is a freely invented story that functions the same way as the similitude and has all of its attributes. The parable is like a similitude in that the "resemblance"

refs the hearer/reader to an external reality; the difference is that the parable is an imaginary story that takes place in the past. Jülicher considers this form to be a *fable,* but because that term is often confused with an animal story, he uses the term *parable* instead (I.92–111). The story of the Sower is a parable (Mt 13:1–9; Mk 4:1–9; Lk 8:4–8).

3. *Example Story (Erzählung)*—The example story, like the parable, is a freely invented story. It differs from the above two categories, however, because it doesn't just refer to an external reality; it is an actual illustration of the reality/truth it is meant to demonstrate (I.112–15). The parable of the Good Samaritan (Lk 10:30–37) is an *example story* that embodies an illustration of the general moral principle of loving one's neighbor. This loving compassion has the highest worth in the eyes of God, and even a Samaritan is approved as neighbor—rather than the selfish Temple officials—if he acts compassionately (II.596). Previous allegorical interpretations of this parable completely missed the point. The specific places named in the parable, for example, do not affect its meaning because Jerusalem does not symbolize "paradise" and Jericho is not "the world." The two cities simply give local flavor to this example story, and the attempt to find symbolism in the smallest details is not only ill advised, but doomed to fail. Instead, Jülicher contends, we should seek out the one basic point of comparison—the neighborly actions of the Samaritan—to understand the meaning of the parable as Jesus intended it (II.585–98).

As is to be expected in such a seminal work, Jülicher's significant contributions also incorporate many flaws. Jülicher's slighting of the Jewish context of Jesus' parables to utilize a more Aristotelian perspective was severely criticized (see chapter 4 below). His insistence that a parable has only one "point" and his claim that there is an "essential" (*wesentlich;* I.52) difference between simile and metaphor seem overdrawn.[2] Some scholars also argue that his rigorous exclusion of allegorical elements in the original parables of Jesus is exaggerated (see chapter 7 below), but modern parable scholarship would never completely resuscitate the allegorical method.

Historical-Eschatological Approaches

Jülicher insisted that Jesus' central message was the kingdom of God, an opinion shared by most subsequent scholars, although vigorous debate ensued concerning the nature of that kingdom (see chapter 7 below). C. H. Dodd entered this debate during his Shaffer Lectures at Yale Divinity School in 1935, which resulted in his classic work *The Parables of the Kingdom.*[3] Dodd contends that the eschatological dimensions of Jesus' message about the kingdom of God are essential to understanding his parables. This question is directly related to Dodd's primary area of interest: What was the original intention of a given parable in its historical setting (7, 23)?

Dodd's approach means that parables have to be understood as Jesus told them in their original life setting *(Sitz-im-Leben).* Thus Dodd spends an entire chapter clarifying what happened during the transmission of the parables. Using the Parable of the Talents as an example (Mt 25:14–30; Lk 19:12–27), Dodd sets out to demonstrate that parables actually have three *Sitze-im-Leben:* the historical Jesus, the early church, and the gospel authors. In the first stage, as told by Jesus, the parable of the Talents was aimed toward persons who sought "personal security in a meticulous observance of the Law" and sought to lead such persons "to see their conduct in its true light" (112). Therefore the parable arose out of a concrete situation in the ministry of Jesus. In the service of the early Christian community, however, the parable became an explanation of the maxim that is also found in Mk 4:25: "For to those who have more will be given; and to those who have nothing, even what they have will be taken away." The tendency at this stage of development in the tradition was for parables to be elaborated into general maxims for the guidance of the church (110). Finally, in the hands of the gospel authors, this parable developed an eschatological theme.[4] In the contexts of both Matthew and Luke, the return of the master/nobleman now becomes the return of Christ, and the parable is well on its way to becoming an allegory (113). Dodd thus concludes that sometimes layers of interpretation have to be removed from the gospel parables to "make an attempt to reconstruct its original setting in the life of Jesus" (84).

Dodd's "original setting"—as is every attempt to postulate an original specific historical event—is a hypothetical, reconstructed context. We cannot recover, with certainty, the "original utterance" of Jesus in a particular situation during his ministry. At the very least, a parable could have been "originally" uttered in several different contexts, which complicates the already impossible task of recovering "the words of Jesus" in a specific, particularized historical setting (see chapter 7 below). On the other hand, we need to make use of the historical information that we have, and Dodd's reconstructions take their place among many plausible others.

In addition, Dodd's search for the historical context also needs to be affirmed in its insistence on trying to interpret the parables in their first-century contexts. Perhaps a better word would be *realism,* and the realism of the parables' first-century context is also intimately connected to their existence as works of art. Thus Dodd rejects the claim that his historical interest was reductionistic,[5] and his classic definition of *parable* perhaps illustrates this best: "At its simplest the parable is a metaphor or simile drawn from nature or common life, arresting the hearer by its vividness or strangeness, and leaving the mind in sufficient doubt about its precise application to tease it into active thought" (16).[6]

Dodd contends that parables are the natural expression of a mind that sees truth in concrete pictures (16); thus parables are consistently and realistically true to life: "Each similitude or story is a perfect picture of something that can be observed in the world of our experience" (19). If an element of the story is surprising, that is the point of the parable—that such actions *are* surprising, such as a worker's reaction to an employer who pays the same wage for one hour's work as for twelve. Yet, overall, the parables convey a "singularly complete and convincing picture" of peasant life in first-century Palestine (19–20).

Joachim Jeremias, who wrote perhaps the most influential work on the parables,[7] acknowledges his indebtedness to Dodd's work: "Professor Dodd's book has opened a new era in the study of parables; although differences of opinion with regard to some details may exist, yet it is unthinkable that there should ever be any retreat from the essential lines laid down by Dodd…" (9). Jeremias's work, however, signaled a new chapter in this era inaugurated by Dodd because of Jeremias's more vigorous "attempt to arrive at the earliest attainable form of Jesus' parabolic teaching" (9).

Jeremias divides his study into two main sections: (a) a thorough investigation of the various "principles of transformation," that is, the numerous ways the early church altered the parables, and (b) a recovery of the main themes of the parables in their initial context during the ministry of the historical Jesus. On one hand, Jeremias states: "We stand right before Jesus when reading his parables" (12). On the other hand, the parables confront us with a "difficult problem": They had undergone a certain amount of reinterpretation. Jeremias's attempt to recapture Jesus from the clutches of the early church is made possible, he claims, because parables were not altered by a random, haphazard process. Instead we find "certain definite principles of transformation" (or "laws": *Gesetze,* 23), and once those principles are illuminated, we can eliminate the husks of reinterpretation and see the kernels of Jesus' parables once again.[8]

Once we reach (Jeremias's version of) the original parables of Jesus, their messages come shining through and center on a few basic ideas. At their heart, the parables stress the eschatological nature of Jesus' preaching. In other words, the kingdom of God is in the *process of realization* in the ministry of Jesus (230)—the day of salvation was at hand. This eschatological urgency leads to the stress on the absolute necessity for immediate repentance.[9] In addition, the parables are often weapons of controversy. Jesus created them as spontaneous responses to the challenges of his opponents to justify his words, defend his actions, or attack/challenge the words/actions of his opponents. Jeremias includes a discussion of the Good Samaritan in the category "Realized Discipleship" (198–219) and declares that the parable depicts the "boundless love" that a disciple of Jesus should have (202). He explores the parable's teasingly open-ended aspects, such as possible motivations for why the priest and the Levite pass by the robbed man lying at the side of the road. Then he asserts, based on the triadic structure often found in popular stories, that the listeners were waiting for a third person to come by—"an Israelite layman" (204). Instead Jesus uses the example of a hated Samaritan to demonstrate the unlimited nature of the duty of love. This example story illustrates that no one should be beyond the range of charity: "The law of love called him [i.e., the lawyer] to be ready at any time to give his life for another's need" (205).

Jeremias's achievement should not be underestimated; his study set the standard for virtually all subsequent investigations of the parables *as told by the historical Jesus*. His influence can still be clearly seen in the work of the Jesus Seminar, a group that has published their view of the authenticity of Jesus' parables.[10] Yet we should also not forget that these reconstructions and the interpretations based on them are hypothetical. For example, Jeremias's personal religious views influence his conception of the life setting of Jesus' ministry.[11] The "principles of transformation" also make the process from the parables of the historical Jesus to the parables of the Synoptic Gospels appear much simpler than it actually was. This transmission did not follow "natural laws" like an experiment in a test tube; we simply cannot "scientifically" postulate cause and effect the way Jeremias tends to do.[12] The actual processes seem to be rather irregular and much more complex than Jeremias suggests. In addition, Jeremias's almost exclusive concern with historical issues leads him to neglect the literary qualities of the parables themselves. For him, interpretation of the parables is a means to an end: reconstructing the message of the historical Jesus.

Redaction-Critical Approaches

The primary concern of Dodd and Jeremias was to recover the life setting of the historical Jesus. Jeremias, especially, also discusses the life setting of the early church, but he tends to disregard, in practice, the active role of the gospel authors. The primary focus of redaction criticism, on the other hand, is to analyze the theological perspectives of an author by investigating the compositional and editorial practices employed. At the very least, redaction criticism demonstrates that gospel authors were far from passive conveyors, mere collectors, or editors of traditions. Instead, the authors were theologians who selected, arranged, shaped, elaborated, and interpreted those traditions from their own theological perspectives.

Jack Kingsbury's redactional study of the parables in Matthew 13 is a case in point.[13] He assumes that just as Jesus employed parables to meet the demands of his situation, Matthew[14] redacted the parables he received to meet the situation of his church. Kingsbury contends that "Matthew's Church," whose members were of both Jewish and Gentile origins, looked on itself as the "true Israel." At the same time, it was in close, agonistic contact with Pharisaic Judaism (11).

In a move representative of redaction critics, Kingsbury argues that this situation in Matthew's church is reflected in the construction of the gospel. Matthew depicts Jesus' ministry to the Jews and the ensuing ministries of his 12 disciples (i.e., Mt 10:1–8). The "Jews," however, reject these ministries, and the great "turning point" in Matthew's Gospel comes in reaction to that rejection: The Matthean Jesus turns against the Jews (130) and subsequently speaks to them, not openly as before, but in enigmatic parables. At the same time, Jesus turns *toward* his twelve disciples, who are the true people of God (13:10–17). For Matthew, however, this "turning" is not past history; it has continuing relevance for his church because it is experiencing a similar "rejection," especially by contemporary Pharisaic Judaism. Kingsbury thus argues that the parables of Matthew 13 in their present literary context portray the author's theological objective: The twelve disciples (and the church) comprehend Jesus' parabolic mysteries of the kingdom of Heaven, but the recalcitrant "Jews" do not understand these enigmatic "riddles" and therefore stand under God's judgment (135).

Redaction criticism partly directs one's attention back to the parables as they appear in the texts. This makes a hypothetical reconstruction of the "original" parables not as necessary, and it can lead to a closer examination of how parables fit into the structure of the gospel narratives. Charles Carlston's study, *The Parables of the Triple Tradition,*[15] illustrates this very well. Carlston sets out to study the parables of Mark, and the variant forms of them in Matthew and Luke, as part of the *text* (xi). Carlston praises the work of Dodd and Jeremias but disagrees with aspects of their "single-minded," hypothetical reconstructions of the historical Jesus. A greater danger for Carlston, however, is the neglect, if not depreciation, of the contributions of the gospel authors, who are significant theologians in their own right.

Carlston proceeds by examining the sixteen parables found in Mark, first in their Matthean settings and then in their Lukan settings. Then he explores the Markan parables in the literary setting of Mark itself. Carlston is a superb redaction critic with an eye for detail, and his keen observations make clear that sometimes, at the very least, we cannot reconstruct the specific form in which Jesus spoke a particular parable.

Carlston's perspective can be succinctly summarized by his approach to the difficult saying in Mark 4:10–12—that Jesus spoke in parables, *so that* some may *not* perceive, understand, and be forgiven. Matthew almost completely transforms this saying

(Mt 13:10–17). His modifications of Mark change their purpose and soften this Markan "hardening theory" almost into nonexistence (7). The result is a double-edged beatitude concerning the understanding/believing disciples and the uncomprehending/ unbelieving outsiders (8). Luke, on the other hand, greatly abbreviates the saying (8:9–10) but, like Matthew, renders it innocuous in various ways (57). The saying becomes much more individualized and ethicized so that a "mere husk" remains of Mark's hardening theory (57). Finally, Carlston notes that Mark's entire Gospel depicts a theological solution to the problem of unbelief: God hardened the unbelieving heart, and, to a lesser degree, the disciples share in the general blindness (108). Carlston's discussion ends with his own double-edged analysis: It is very difficult to see this saying as coming from the historical Jesus (105–8), but Mark's presentation is not just "a simple misunderstanding of little theological value." It contains a warning to us not to underestimate these issues in simplistic intellectual or moral terms (109).

To sum up, redaction criticism made many advances, but despite its productive move back toward the texts, it still focuses primarily on the gospel authors, or, more specifically, on the author's specific historical situation behind what is supposedly reflected by the text—such as Kingsbury's detailed theory of the close interaction of Matthew's "community" with "Pharisaic Judaism." I would argue, however, that such specific historical reconstructions, whether of events in the ministry of Jesus (e.g., Dodd, Jeremias) or of situations in the communities of the evangelists (e.g., Kingsbury), attempt to peer through the murky window clouded by the process of communication. Ideology, cultural and social locations, and many other factors distance us from the authors' particular historical situations. Our hypothetical reconstructions are complicated by the tendentious nature of the primary sources themselves. We should approach these reconstructions with appreciation, but also with mature skepticism and critical acumen.

Parables and the "New Hermeneutic"

Ernst Fuchs inaugurated the New Hermeneutic approach to the parables, which is a conscious continuation of, but departure from, the approach taken by his teacher, Rudolph Bultmann. Bultmann, perhaps the premier New Testament scholar of the twentieth century, wanted to communicate the Christian message *(kerygma)* to modern persons. Writing in Germany in 1941, he saw a great hermeneutical (i.e., interpretive) chasm between the "mythological" language of the New Testament and the "technological" language of twentieth-century humans. He proposed to bridge this gulf by "demythologizing" the language of the New Testament, specifically by interpreting its language in a mode common to both languages: the concern for "authentic" existence. Here Bultmann is indebted to the existentialist philosophy of Martin Heidegger, but whereas Heidegger saw authentic existence as a resolute decision to live life more fully and authentically in light of the inescapable reality of death, Bultmann saw authentic existence as an affirmation of faith that comes in response to an encounter with the Word of God. This faith, however, is not in the historical Jesus; instead it is in the Christ of the *kerygma.*[16]

At this point Fuchs differentiates himself from Bultmann's thought. Fuchs was one of the leaders of the "New Quest" of the historical Jesus. This New Quest began among former students of Bultmann because they were concerned that his approach postulated too much discontinuity between the historical Jesus and the Christ of faith. Bultmann, for example, tenaciously refused to speak of the historical Jesus' self-understanding or thought-processes.[17] Fuchs, on the other hand, speaks of parables as verbalizing Jesus' personal understanding of existence, not only to the original hearers but even to modern interpreters.[18] This process is critical, as Fuchs states very clearly: "I am convinced that the question of the immediate meaning of Jesus for us cannot be answered apart from the question of the 'historical' Jesus."[19]

Fuchs is not talking about "facts" in the sense of specific historical events in the life and ministry of Jesus. Instead, this "New Quest" is aided and abetted by the "New Hermeneutic": Parables are "language events" in which Jesus' understanding of his own existence, situation, and faith "enters language," and his understanding of existence is still available for us to share. The faith of Jesus, the decision he made for God and God's kingdom, comes to us today through the language event of parables. The literary form of the parables promotes this performative aspect: They function primarily as similitudes—as analogies or indirect speech—in that their point of comparison (between, for example, the kingdom of God and the story told in a parable) can enable the faith journey of Jesus to become that of the believer.

One of Fuchs's students, Eta Linnemann, wrote a book on the parables that made this complex approach, according to Fuchs, "completely intelligible."[20] Linnemann explains that a parable is a form of communication, a dialogue between narrator and listener. As such, it is an urgent endeavor, because the narrator wants to do much more than just impart information. The teller of a parable wants to influence the other person, to win agreement. The parable is the means of overcoming any resistance the hearer might have.

A successful parable is an "event" in two ways: (a) it decisively alters the situation by creating a possibility of agreement that did not exist before, and (b) it compels the one addressed to make a decision—although the outcome of the decision is completely up to the listener. The deeper the opposition that exists between the speaker and the listener, the more significant the decision to be made, and Jesus' parables speak to oppositions that "reach right into the depths of existence" (31). Jesus, by compelling this momentous decision through his parable-telling, gives his opponents the possibility of achieving a "new life," making a change of existence, and understanding themselves "from the depths up" (31). Because this "language event" is subject to historical change (e.g., we do not stand in the same situation as the original listeners), it cannot be transmitted to us directly. Yet it can be made intelligible in exposition and in preaching. Preaching, in fact, repeats the event that happened to the hearers of the first parables because it is grounded in what Jesus did when he risked his word (33).

Linnemann's discussion of the parable of the Good Samaritan illustrates this approach very well. First she retells the parable with a running commentary (51–55), an exposition that is geared toward making the parable intelligible. The meaning of Jesus' answer, she claims, is that Jesus calls a person to change from the position where the world is controlled by law that strives for completeness and to move toward "authentic living" (55–56). So the story of the Good Samaritan emphatically demonstrates that what really matters is to act as the Samaritan did—to let ourselves be governed completely by the needs of the person before us.

To a certain extent, both Fuchs and Linnemann retain an interest in a historical understanding of the text. In addition, they see the parables as either the medium for conveying Jesus' understanding of the world (Fuchs) or as Jesus' verbal bridge to his opponents (Linnemann). The practitioners of the New Hermeneutic, though, even with their concern for literary form and language, did not really examine adequately the literary aspects of the parables. Their concern with the hearer of the parable was indeed a step forward, but, in their concern to respond to questions of contemporary existence, they (re)expressed the parables in existentialist terms and utilized the dominant model of the sermon. What remained undone was the construction of a literary method that would serve as a more solid foundation for examining parables as parables. That literary path would be blazed by such scholars as Amos Wilder, Dan Via, Robert Funk, and John Dominic Crossan.

2
The Emergence of Literary Approaches to the Parables

A seismic shift in parable study began in the United States during the 1960s and 1970s initiated by what came to be known as the American School. In many ways, this shift was a further development of historical-critical approaches, but it also represented a significant change in orientation and methodology. In brief, parable study during this energetic era focused more on parables as literary works of art. At the forefront of these creative innovations, and in the middle of those often tempestuous discussions, stood Amos Wilder.[1]

Aesthetic-Rhetorical Criticism

Amos Wilder seemed uniquely qualified both to inspire and influence a generation of parable scholars.[2] His credentials as a New Testament scholar were unquestioned, and as a literary critic he provided indispensable insights in the very area in which current discussion was deficient: parables as literary works of art. In addition, he had the heart, soul, and imagination of a poet, which allowed him to bring the methodological "dry bones" of literary criticism to vibrant, flesh-and-blood life.

Wilder situates his study of the parables in the context of his larger vision concerning the nature of language in general and the language of the New Testament in particular. His chapter on the parables in *The Language of the Gospel*[3] is only eighteen pages long, but it established the parameters for discussions for years to come. He begins by disagreeing with the opinion that the Synoptic parables are merely devices to hold an audience's attention or only a colorful means of illustration. Instead, there is "something in the nature of the Gospel" that evokes this rhetoric (79): Jesus' message of the imminent denouement of the world; twelve o'clock is beginning to strike.

For Wilder, the parables exhibit such tremendous variety and flexibility that it is almost misleading to use the term *parable* because it suggests a nonexistent "single pattern" (81). Some are, for instance, "example stories," such as the parable of the Good Samaritan. But other parables—as extended, symbolic narrative images—reveal rather than exemplify. Wilder stresses this revelatory image because Jesus, as do the prophets and apocalypticists, uses extended images to mediate reality and life. Influenced by contemporary literary-critical discussions of metaphor—particularly the work of the poet and literary critic Ezra Pound[4]—Wilder contends that a metaphor imparts an "image with a certain shock to the imagination which directly conveys a vision of what is signified" (80). The hearer participates in this reality and, in fact, is "invaded" by it (92).[5]

Jesus' vision as mediated by his parables is human, realistic, and secular. Even though parables sometimes evoke images of the Hebrew Bible, the dominant outlook is not "religious" per se, but they achieve their impact by an immediate, realistic authenticity: "In the parable of the Lost Sheep the shepherd is an actual shepherd and not a flash-back to God as the Shepherd of Israel..." (81). These sharply focused snapshots of human life reveal something exceedingly important about their author. They provide a vista from which we can perceive that, in the very human, everyday existence vividly portrayed in the parables, human destiny itself is at stake.

This incarnational vision of everyday existence is a spring-board to something even more important—the "meaning or appli-cation." But Wilder insists that even here there is no "great leap out of the world" (82). Instead, Jesus leads his listeners to make a judgment and to come to a decision; the parables are profound dramas portraying life at the root of its existence and involving the full range of human experience.[6]

Wilder is so impressed by the literary form of and the vision evoked by Jesus' parables that he sees them as having a "formal uniqueness" and an unparalleled depth of morality in their por-trayal of humanity and the enigma of existence (83–85). Here Wilder encounters a possible stumbling block. How can a person proclaiming an acute eschatological crisis attain such "rhetorical perfection?" An apparently "fanatical" apocalyptic visionary seems to have almost nothing in common with the humanist who utters the parables (85–87). In Wilder's view, however, Jesus transcends such dichotomies, and he, in fact, uses and brings together these disparate elements in his teaching.[7]

Wilder is quite concerned with the historical Jesus, and this can be seen in his discussion concerning the parables of the king-dom (90–96). Standing on the shoulders of Dodd and Jeremias, Wilder argues that the parables must be extricated from their gospel contexts, and the "original form" must be reconstructed (90).[8] He does not offer a program for recovering the original parables but asserts that true parables of Jesus have a "tight form" that resists change. The acid test is whether they have the "focus and depth" characteristic of the original, authentic parables of Jesus (91).

Once we accomplish this reconstruction, Wilder contends, we can see the parables from the viewpoint of Jesus' own situa-tion, and only then do their real power and authority emerge: "It is Jesus' own faith that paints in the feature of the great harvest" (93). We see the intensity of his vision, for example, in the parable of the Sower, which expresses his conviction that faith and expec-tation are identified with daily life and God's operation there. Like the first disciples, to find the true power and joy of Jesus' metaphors, "we must identify ourselves with that inner secret of Jesus' faith and faithfulness" (93).

Wilder sees the historical Jesus as synthesizing elements from many tributaries and as uniting in himself many roles, such as prophet, lawgiver, seer, and sage (86). As such, Jesus holds together many divergent perspectives and transcends those roles. In particular, his intense eschatological consciousness is held in tension with his poetic, "secular" vision. Similarly, Wilder's literary and historical interests bring together many divergent perspectives and tendencies. Wilder makes a significant advance on the work of such scholars as Jeremias through his analysis of the literary qualities of the parables themselves, but his study still contains a similar limitation: These reconstructions of the parables as told by the historical Jesus are hypothetical—as are the interpretations based upon them.

The Parable as Metaphor

Robert Funk entered the metaphorical door opened by Wilder and furthered the study of parables as narrative metaphors by focusing not on parable as direct communication *about* something, but as a language event that reshaped the world of the listener to the point where a judgment was necessary about the everyday world. Thus, like Wilder, Funk stressed the "secularity" of the parables and studied the function of poetic language, as well as the formal features of the parables.

Funk forcefully discusses these conceptions in a chapter entitled "The Parable as Metaphor" in his book *Language, Hermeneutic, and the Word of God.*[9] Here Funk combines Dodd's definition of a parable as metaphor (see chapter 1 above) with Wilder's insight that metaphor "is a bearer of the reality to which it refers."

He distills four essential points from Dodd's definition: (1) the parable is a metaphor or simile which may (a) remain simple, (b) be elaborated into a picture, or (c) be expanded into a story;

(2) the metaphor or simile is drawn from nature or common life; (3) the metaphor arrests the hearer by its vividness or strangeness; and (4) the application is left imprecise to tease the hearers into making their own applications (133).

The fourth aspect marks Funk's starting point: "[T]he parable is not closed, so to speak, until the listener is drawn into it as a participant" (133). This assertion has several implications. First, Funk assumes, as Dodd and Jeremias did before him, that few if any of the parables were given applications by the historical Jesus. Second, the applications were appended by the early church and/or the gospel authors and may not agree with the intent of the historical Jesus. Third, because parables are open ended, it is impossible to delineate in didactic language what parables mean. In fact, even if the original setting(s) of a parable could be recovered, because Jesus' original audience was diverse and different listeners "complete" the parable in different ways, the entire idea of *one* "original meaning" is fallacious. To give a parable one particular application—whether done by the earliest Christian communities, the gospel authors, or scholars today—is to close off the possibility of the listener's participation in the parable itself (135, 149–52). The parable as metaphor thus cannot have just one point (*pace* Jülicher). Even Jesus' original audiences, as well as all subsequent audiences, create as many "points as there were situations into which they are spoken" (151).

Central to Funk's claims about parables are his views as to their nature as metaphors. Funk draws a significant distinction between *simile* and *metaphor* that was left undistinguished in Dodd's original definition of *parable*. In brief, a simile clarifies the less known by use of the better known in an illustrative fashion: "A is *like* B." A metaphor, on the other hand, has an element of comparison, but it functions in a completely different way because metaphor juxtaposes two discrete and not entirely compatible elements: "A *is* B." This juxtaposition is "creative of meaning" and induces a vision that "cannot be conveyed by prosaic or discursive speech" (137). The metaphor confronts us; it produces an impact upon the imagination; it is the bearer of reality. The importance of this move should not be overlooked. Funk completely reverses the conclusion of Jülicher by saying that similes/parables are extended metaphors and are *not* extended comparisons. The "meaning" of a parable is inherent in its metaphorical structure and unfolding images, a metaphorical process that transforms a reader.[10]

Funk then discusses the "realism" of the parables from Dodd's definition (see chapter 1 above; cf. Wilder's "secularity"). This realism, when paired with the parables' "strangeness," seems paradoxical, but Funk reaffirms Wilder's insistence that this combination demonstrates that one's destiny is at stake in one's everyday existence. The unexpected turn in many parables, however, looks through the commonplace to a new view of reality. The hearers, when shocked to find their familiar world turned inside out, must choose to be "illuminated by the metaphor, or reject the call and abide with the conventional" (162).

A clear instance of the effect of Funk's approach can be seen in his disagreement with the prevalent assumption that the Good Samaritan parable is an example story.[11] In his view, the opening sentence of the parable illustrates its "everydayness," but the Samaritan's introduction produces a "primary shock" (212–13). The portrayal of the Samaritan is realistic, but the surprising turn of events shatters the realism. The juxtaposition of these two "logics" turns the Samaritan—and the parable—into a metaphor (213). As a result, Funk argues in a later article,[12] the hearer is caught up into the story as a participant and identifies with the victim in the ditch (79–80). This means that the parable is not illustrative of what it means to be a good neighbor; rather the "meaning" of the parable "occurs" as the auditors take up roles in the story and play out the drama. Because the parable is perpetually unfinished, it does not determine the outcome, and responses vary from person to person and from time to time. Yet Funk surmises that the parable suggests that, in the kingdom of God, mercy always comes to those who have no right to expect it or to resist it, and that mercy always comes as a surprise (80).[13]

The Parable as Aesthetic Object

During the same period of time in which Funk was developing his mode of interpretation, Dan Via investigated parables as "aesthetic objects."[14] Via begins with a four-pronged critique of the historical method presupposed from Jülicher to Jeremias: (1) the gospels are "non-biographical" in nature, so one cannot determine in exactly what concrete situations parables were originally uttered; (2) the "severely historical approach" ignores the basic human element in the parables; (3) the historical approach threatens to leave the parables in the past with nothing to say for the present; (4) the historical approach ignores the inherent aesthetic function of parables as works of art.[15]

Via responds to the limitations of historical interpretation with an assertion that parables are aesthetic objects—carefully organized, self-contained, coherent literary compositions. The beginning point of study, therefore, must be the parables themselves and the structure of connections in their literary patterns. Such an approach frees the interpreter to see that these fictitious literary works are "autonomous"—virtually independent of the author. They reveal things that cannot be traced to the author's biography or environment. Here Via crosses a critical, methodological Rubicon. Because parables are autonomous works of art, we can analyze the understanding of human existence inherent in their literary form and content with virtually no reference to their original historical context: "The only important consideration is the internal meaning of the work itself" (77). Historical factors should be taken into account only insofar as demanded by the narrative.

Via goes on to argue that because parables are aesthetic in nature they are not as "time-conditioned" as other biblical texts and therefore not in need of as much "translation" to make them understandable to modern persons. In addition, there are some elements in all aesthetic objects that are "untranslatable." Via thus concludes that the gap between the first and modern hearers of the parables is smaller than with other kinds of texts, and that first-century hearers "were no more able to translate them completely into other terms than we are" (32–33).

As the subtitle of the book intimates, Via merges his literary analysis with the existential approach of the New Hermeneutic. Via perceives parables as language events that introduce new possibilities into the situations of their hearers. Parables offer a new way of understanding, *and* they call for a judgment: Hearers have to decide between their old understanding and the new one that confronts them in the parable (53–54). The critical difference between Via and such scholars as Fuchs and Linnemann emerges as he explores how the nature of the parable as language event is intricately related to its internal, aesthetic patterns, connections, and functions (55, 57). It is in this internal pattern of connections and functions that their "meaning" is to be found.

Via justifies his literary analysis through a number of features common to narrative fiction, beginning with the standard twofold division of "basic plot movements": *comedy* and *tragedy*.[16] In comedy there is an upward movement toward well-being and the inclusion of the protagonist into a new or renewed society. In tragedy the plot falls toward catastrophe, and the protagonist becomes isolated from society (96). So the parable of the Prodigal Son is a "comic parable," and the parable of the Talents is a "tragic parable." In both cases, definite existential motifs can be discerned. The Prodigal, for example, suggests that human beings are capable of recognizing who and where they are once their legalistic understanding is shattered by unexpected forgiveness (174). The parable of the Talents, on the other hand, demonstrates that "the refusal to risk and the concomitant inability to hold oneself responsible become unfaith" (120).[17]

The Varying Legacies of Wilder, Funk, and Via

Other scholars built upon the insights of Wilder, Funk, and Via but with widely varying trajectories. Sallie McFague, in her book *Speaking in Parables,*[18] for example, argues that parables are most closely associated with the genres of poem, novel, and autobiography because these literary forms address the ways metaphor operates in language, belief, and life. McFague emphasizes the nontransferability of the parabolic metaphor,[19] but she seeks analogies between the metaphorical work of the parable and the story of Jesus. In this way the parables become models of theological reflection: Jesus' parables insist on uniting language, belief, and life, and therefore they can address people's lives in their totality (3).

Mary Ann Tolbert, in her *Perspectives on the Parables,* investigates the parables as "literary texts with a certain timeless dimension rather than as historical artifacts of a long dead culture" (13).[20] Tolbert focuses primarily on the theory of signs in semiotics, but she also presents a rhetorical analysis of their openness ("polyvalence") as metaphor, which makes them so amenable to multiple interpretations.[21] Tolbert observes that competent scholars, even using essentially the same methods, arrive at equally valid, though different, interpretations of the same parable (30). She contends that this difference is inherent in the parabolic form itself: The structure of a parable does not generate "a meaning"; instead it provides basic constraints and possibilities within which a variety of meanings may be perceived.

Thus, according to Tolbert, a parable requires the reader to participate in the creation of meaning. Therefore the meaning lies partially outside the text itself in the dynamic interaction between narrative and reader, the text and a context. Because interpreters must provide "some material" out of their own experiences and concerns, Tolbert concludes that there need not be a single, normative context for interpretation. Thus Tolbert's perspective is an even more radical critique of the almost exclusive concern of scholars such as Dodd and Jeremias to place the parables of Jesus into their "original" first-century context. Instead, interpreters should affirm and even exploit the flexibility of the parables by choosing interpretive contexts that reflect contemporary concerns while preserving the integrity of the stories themselves (71, 94).[22]

James Breech seeks to recover the "original Jesus" by perceiving parables as a window to Jesus' understanding of human existence.[23] Breech limits his study to a core of parables that he considers authentic and then reconstructs their "original form." He claims that the distinctive elements in the sayings and parables of Jesus have a structural similarity to the recognition of the "actual other" in works by such authors as Fyodor Dostoevsky and J. D. Salinger. All of these works advocate a "hyperindividualism" that is committed to "someone or something beyond one's self" (112). Through this commitment each person can find his or her own highly particular way to live with genuineness and integrity. The action of the stories, Breech believes, can be grouped into two categories: "Photodramatic" parables limit themselves to the external descriptions of characters and report *visible* actions; "phonodramatic" parables, on the other hand, describe what people *do* and *say,* by reporting *visible* actions and *audible* words (66).[24]

The Brief Reign of Structuralism

The first meeting of the Society of Biblical Literature's Seminar on the Parables (1973) focused on "A Structuralist Approach to the Parables."[25] Structuralism is in part an intensification of New Criticism, an approach that emphasizes intricate attention to the text itself, but it differs from the Formalist nature of New Criticism by seeking structures that are not apparent on the "surface level" of narratives. Structuralism focuses on the structure of language itself.[26] It seeks to penetrate beneath surface patterns to disclose the "deep structure" that a particular story shares with other narratives. So structuralism does not analyze in any real depth, for example, the content of a story. Instead it focuses on the "meaning effect" of a text and how it is produced; it searches for the general properties that generate specific texts.[27]

In his *Semeia* article,[28] Dan Via adopts the structuralist model of Greimas, as developed by Roland Barthes. Via distinguishes between two levels of narrative: *story* (a created world of events and persons) and *discourse* (a word spoken by a narrator to a hearer). The story level can be further divided into plot (sequential analysis) and *actants* (the function, role, or status of a participant in the action). Via's *actantiel* analysis sees the *actant* Samaritan as wanting to communicate healing to the *actant* traveler. The Samaritan is aided by the *actants* oil, wine, donkey, and innkeeper. Even the robbers "aid" the Samaritan's quest by creating the situation in which he can show compassion. The priest and Levite, at the very least, are "opposites" (112). In its narrative context of Luke 10:25–27, Via envisions Jesus as wanting to aid the lawyer by communicating the meaning of "neighbor" (113).

As William Beardslee notes, structural analysis requires a special vocabulary and a diagramming system that make it forbidding to the uninitiated nonspecialist.[29] On one hand, structuralist approaches often leave nonstructuralist interpreters disappointed because they do not really further our understanding of the parables themselves.[30] On the other hand, literary criticism has moved into various "poststructuralist" perspectives, including deconstruction and reader-response criticism.

Conclusion

Now that scholars had begun to focus on parables as literary works of art, the parables were seen in a much different light. Scholars such as Amos Wilder and Robert Funk reversed Jülicher's contention that similes/parables are expanded comparisons by arguing that parables are extended metaphors. Another important shift occurred, however. Although these scholars, as previous scholars had done, almost always remove parables from their gospel contexts and use the tools of historical criticism to recreate their "original forms," they now also primarily utilize literary criticism to try to understand parables' natural function as language in the new setting of modern interpretations.[31] Thus new methods and skills, such as linguistic and structural emphases, are applied within these literary analyses and interpretations. But, as we shall see in the following chapters, much about the language of and about the parables remained to be explored. To these studies we now turn.

3
Fully Developed Literary
Approaches to the Parables

A new era had begun with the emergence of literary approaches to the parables, but these insights had not yet been applied, in a programmatic way, to the entire parable corpus or to key parables within a particular gospel. This chapter analyzes how earlier works on the literary aspects of the parables began to bear fruit in the works of other scholars. John Dominic Crossan is the primary example because he pulls together the insights of his predecessors and furthers their work with innovative insights from contemporary literary criticism. John Drury and others, on the other hand, also represent an important turning point; they return the parables to their gospel contexts but now examine them afresh with a literary sensitivity to how parables function as narratives within larger narratives.

John Dominic Crossan

Crossan's complex odyssey in and his prolific contributions to parable study clearly demonstrate not only his versatility, but also the evolution of his thought. In his book *In Parables: The Challenge of the Historical Jesus,*[1] he examines the "historical Jesus," not in the sense of his religion, faith, or self-understanding, but in the sense of the language of Jesus—specifically that of "the reconstructed parabolic complex" (xiii).

The distinction Crossan makes between parable and allegory is crucial for his thesis. He compares *allegory*—which expresses the intelligible—and *symbol*—which expresses the inexpressible. Parables, for Crossan, are metaphoric language that, unlike allegory, cannot be paraphrased in conceptual terms. Just as Samuel Taylor Coleridge emphasized participation in the referent as the heart of metaphor, Crossan stresses that parable as poetic metaphor creates participation in the metaphor's referent because one can only experience its reality by risking entrance into it (10–16). Crossan then argues that not only do the parables of Jesus reflect the temporality of Jesus' experience of God and establish the historicity of Jesus' response to the kingdom, they "create and establish the historical situation of Jesus himself" (32). In other words, Jesus was not crucified for speaking parables, but for ways of acting that resulted from the experience of God presented in the parables.

These poetic metaphors, Crossan asserts, portray a "permanent eschatology," the continuous presence of God as the one who challenges world and repeatedly shatters its complacency. This kingdom of God and its parables manifest an *advent* of a radical new world of possibility, a *reversal* of ordinary expectations and the past, and a call to *action* as an expression of the new world with new possibilities (26–27).[2] Crossan then identifies three "key" parables "which show most clearly this deep structure of the Kingdom's temporality" of advent, reversal, and action (33–34; the Treasure, Mt 13:44; the Pearl, Mt 13:45; and the Great Fish, *Gospel of Thomas* 81:28–82:3).

Crossan's approach is quite evident in his discussion of the Good Samaritan (57–66). First, he rejects the gospel context as unoriginal and therefore useless for interpreting the meaning of Jesus' parable. He then "restores" the structure of the narrative so that he can investigate the "meaning for Jesus." The internal structure of the story and the historical setting of Jesus' time both agree that the story's thrust demands that the hearer respond by saying the contradictory, the impossible, the unspeakable: *Good* Samaritan. The point thus is not that one should help the neighbor in need. When good (priest and Levite) becomes bad, and bad (Samaritan) becomes good, a world is being challenged with a polar reversal, and the leap from this "impossible" literal point to the *metaphorical* point is the real purpose of the literary creation. Metaphorically, the kingdom breaks into human consciousness "just so" (65); it demands the overturning of prior values, set judgments, and established conclusions. The hearer, struggling with the contradictory dualism of Good/Samaritan, is actually experiencing the inbreaking of the kingdom of God in and through this parable (66).

Because Crossan prefers "the Celtic twilight to the Arthurian sunlight," the title and content of his next book, *The Dark Interval,*[3] is not surprising. He utilizes the structuralist models of Claude Lévi-Strauss (as adapted by the anthropologists Elli and Pierre Maranda) and Algirdas Greimas (as modified by Roland Barthes) and asserts that "reality is language" (37). Language is all we have, and "we live in story like fish in the sea" (47). In his pursuit of the question of how God can be experienced in this situation, Crossan argues that the dominant narrative patterns in a culture form the hearer's world of expectation. This myth is in mind whenever any other story is heard, and the hearer naturally notices what fits and doesn't fit between the two stories. Whereas myth establishes world, parable subverts world. Crossan contends that all of Jesus' parables are world-shattering invitations to live without myth. In Crossan's words, parables "are stories which shatter the deep structure of our accepted world and thereby render clear and evident to us the relativity of story itself. They remove our defences and make us vulnerable to God. It is only in such experiences that God can touch us, and only in such moments does the kingdom of God arrive. My own term for this relationship is transcendence" (122).

Crossan's *Raid on the Articulate* juxtaposes sayings and parables of Jesus with works by the Argentine author Jorge Luis

Borges.[4] Both are "literary iconoclasts," parablers who can evoke for us "comic eschatology"—or the permanence of revelation's imminence (169)—and their language is a system of signs constructive of the worlds to which it refers. Time, for example, is "imagination's play" with layers of story "within which and only within which we live, move, and have our being" (137).[5] Crossan's affinity with deconstruction becomes clearer in this book as he emphasizes play, polyvalence, and indeterminacy.

Crossan's next book, *Finding is the First Act,*[6] examines the structures of the parable of the hidden treasure (Mt 13:44) by mapping out its plot options (finding, acting, buying) in comparison with other Jewish treasure stories and an array of "treasure plots" in world folklore. Crossan observes that, in the parable, the finder joyfully gives up everything to obtain the treasure. That, says Jesus, is what the kingdom of God is like. But a dark shadow appears, because if one gives up "all"—and if this "all" is to be taken seriously—then *"one must also give up this parable itself"* (94). One must even give up the advice to give up everything. Crossan concludes that this parable is a "metaparable," a paradoxical artifact that succeeds precisely to the extent it fails: "I will tell you, it says, what the kingdom of God is like. Watch carefully how and as I fail to do so and learn that it cannot be done. Have you seen my failure? If you have, then I have succeeded. And the more magnificent my failure, the greater my success" (120).[7]

In Crossan's *Cliffs of Fall,*[8] he shares Jacques Derrida's belief that all language is metaphoric. Metaphor creates a "void" of meaning that generates the free play of interpretations. Language thus is judged to be polyvalent—it allows no single and definitive reading/hearing to emerge. For Crossan, theology therefore must be seen as devoid of absolutes and of all pretense of knowing any secure reality by which to test other reality claims: "Parable becomes the deconstructive medium par excellence."[9]

Crossan's innovative work radiates brilliant insights. If it is true, as Mary Ann Tolbert suggests, that there is no single, normative context for interpretation and that interpreters should choose contexts that reflect contemporary concerns to exploit the flexibility of the parables, then Crossan's work stands unparalleled. On the other hand, I suggest that part of preserving the integrity of these stories is respecting their literary, cultural, social, and (general) historical contexts. The reader produces meaning, but only by participating in a complex of socially constructed practices.[10] When scholars interpret parables through Freudian theory (Tolbert), Jungian theory (Via), or as if they were composed by Kafka (Crossan), we have traveled very far indeed from first-century Palestine—where an itinerant teacher first spoke these stories—and from the first-century Mediterranean world in which the Gospels were composed.[11]

Bernard Brandon Scott

Brandon Scott's first book[12] consciously works out of the legacy of such scholars as Wilder, Funk, Via, and Crossan but seeks to expand those insights from parables to other forms of Jesus' language. He develops a literary analysis of the historical Jesus' language by arguing that structuralist models developed in parable criticism provide a basis for a coherent insight into Jesus' language as a whole. Language, for Scott, is not "words," but a system of signs. In this way, Jesus' utterances (or "performances") can be explored to discover the underlying grammar (or "structure") of their symbolic organization (2). After Scott develops a descriptive analysis of Jesus' language, he then constructs models to evaluate selected other sayings and deeds of Jesus to analyze whether they result "from the same organizing symbolic world" (3).

Scott sees parables as verbalizations of "Jesus' World" but argues that we can not delineate that "horizon of meaning" with any precision. Our best hope is to develop a "metalanguage" (a language about language) to generate a "unified insight" that reflects this horizon (16–17). Scott first "isolates" a parable from its gospel setting and then attempts to "reconstruct" the parable. Then he analyzes a parable's "underlying narrative structure" (24–25), which leads him to postulate five theses that appear to "form a consistent horizon of parable" (30–32).[13]

For this "underlying structure" of parables, Scott employs Ferdinand de Saussure's distinction between *parole* (a speech act) and *langue* (a linguistic system): Parables are individual *parole* governed by rules of an underlying *langue* (98). For "narrative parables" (parables in which narrative motion dominates) Scott adopts the structuralist *actantiel* model of Greimas. The consistent pattern in these parables is that at least one *actant* is always moved away from an *expected* position in that model to an *unexpected* position (99). For "one-liners" (parables in which intensified insight dominates) Scott utilizes the structuralist model of Claude Lévi-Strauss, in which "an apparently irresoluble opposition between two terms is overcome" by a mediating third term. From those two models and his five theses—and an array of diagrams!—Scott constructs a unified model: a "so-called square of opposition." This model places the "Kingdom of God" at one end and "The Accepted" at the other as a semantic axis that generates the arrangement of images in the parables, just as the rules of grammar generate a sentence (120–21). Finally, Scott applies this model to selected other sayings and deeds of Jesus (127–63).

Scott's magisterial *Hear Then the Parable* exhibits a maturation of his insights.[14] The introductory sections in "Part One: Prolegomena" are essential for understanding Scott's approach. He works through, in detail, his definition of parable: "A parable is a mashal that employs a short narrative fiction to reference a transcendent symbol." Thus he is still accenting the literary, linguistic, and metaphorical aspects of the parables, with an emphasis on the relationship of the parables (as symbols) to the mythological vision of the kingdom of God.[15]

Scott's comprehensive study provides a discussion of the Synoptic parables. He divides the parables into categories structured around three elementary aspects of first-century Mediterranean life: "Family, Village, City, and Beyond" (79–202), "Masters and Servants" (205–98), and "Home and Farm" (301–417). With this "macro classification" in place, Scott devises a consistent strategy that pursues an analysis of each parable in a three-step pattern (redaction, reading, and the kingdom of God).

First, Scott analyzes the function of the parable in its present context(s) in the Synoptics and the *Gospel of Thomas* (each evangelist's "performance" of the parable). The surface structure of a parable, Scott believes, is a critical bridge between the evangelist's performance and Jesus' performance (the "originating" structure).[16] The surface structure can be spotted in the mnemonic features of oral language, such as the use of formulas, chiasmus, and wordplays. Scott probes those surface features and then, for the parables included in more than one gospel, tries to sketch out how the originating structure took form (74–75).

Second, Scott offers his reading of the parable. In this section, he attempts to show how the originating structure and/or the surface structure effects meaning in the interaction between text and reader. Thus Scott's methodology of reading can now be classified as "reception-theory analysis" (or "reader-response criticism"), which endeavors to construct the dynamic of a narrative seeking to structure its own perception and is, in turn, structured by the receiver's response. Scott argues that the fictive, narrative quality of parable bestows on it an independence of its immediate *Sitz-im-Leben,* so we can distinguish two levels of meaning: (a) "situational meaning" is the particular meaning that readers impart to the text depending upon their situation (i.e., a "real reader"); (b) the "second level of literary meaning" concerns textual structuring, a self-referential semantics that supports the first level of meaning. This second level of meaning provides the possibility of both multiple and specific applications in the situation of Jesus, the gospels, and all subsequent readings. The "implied reader" operates at this second level of meaning because the implied reader "is a textual strategy that represents the predispositions necessary for a literary work to exercise its magic."[17]

Third, Scott explores "the parabolic effect" that emerges from the juxtaposition of the parable story and the kingdom of God. In other words, how do narrative and kingdom interact to create parable (76)? In the parable of the Good Samaritan, for example, Scott concludes that to "remain in the story," the hearer "becomes a victim" (i.e., the man in the ditch). This identification *must* occur because there is no other Israelite with whom the hearer can identify and to "identify with the Samaritan is almost impossible" because of the enmity between Jew and Samaritan (199).[18] The parable subverts the effort to order reality into a known hierarchy of priest, Levite, and Israelite because the kingdom of God does not separate insiders from outsiders on the basis of religious categories. Thus the world, with its "sure" arrangement of insiders and outsiders, is no longer an adequate model for predicting the kingdom.

Contextual Readings of the Parables

John Drury consciously positions his work in contrast to the "orthodoxy" that ignores the gospel contexts to reconstruct the "original" parables of Jesus.[19] Drury responds to that orthodoxy by critiquing the idea that modern scholars (e.g., Jeremias) could understand the nature of parable better than the author of Mark (40). Instead, Drury asserts, leaving the parables in their gospel contexts restores their power and sense of drama, so his solution is to "let Mark's theology speak for itself" (42–43). A prime example is how the parable of the Sower foreshadows what "is going to happen in the story yet to come" (51). Drury argues that not only do parables cast light upon the narrative, but they also should be interpreted in light of the narrative (65).

Robert Tannehill views Luke-Acts as a unified literary work with an overarching purpose that provides unity to the complex narrative.[20] Tannehill thus focuses on the internal connections among different parts of the narrative: themes being developed, dropped, and presented again; characters and actions echoing characters and actions in other parts of the story. So Tannehill is primarily concerned with, for example, a parable's function in the total narrative. The interactions between various parts of the narrative help to create meanings for readers, and Tannehill seeks to highlight those concerns in the overall literary design of the narrative (3–5).

Therefore Tannehill discusses the function of the parable of the Good Samaritan only in Luke's narrative. The story in Luke 10:25–37 first affirms (as does 18:18–23) what Jewish leaders and Jesus have in common—their recognition of the commandments of the law. The story, however, goes on to highlight the distinctiveness of Jesus. Jesus insists that if the lawyer really wants to fulfill the commandment, he must act as the Samaritan acted—and in doing so must ignore social and religious barriers. The Lukan Jesus' command touches upon a major problem for the Lukan scribes and Pharisees. Their purity system—and their resulting feelings of superiority—exclude those whom God desires to include, such as tax collectors and sinners (179–81).

Tannehill's analysis is significant because he focuses on how parables function within the Gospel of Luke itself. Within that context, parables further the story's plot development. In addition, the characters in the parables give implicit and explicit commentary on the characters in the narrative. Such approaches to the parables in their literary contexts certainly are not the *only* way to interpret these parables, but they do demonstrate clearly the function of parables as integral elements in the gospel narratives. As Ched Myers argues, parables stand in fundamental relationship to the story as a whole and cannot be properly interpreted apart from it; they function primarily as a kind of "mirror" to assist the reader/hearer.[21]

An analysis of the "mirror-like" functions of parables, from a socio-narratological perspective, is found in my book, *Host, Guest, Enemy, and Friend.*[22] I investigate the enigmatic portrayals of the Pharisees in Luke and Acts and demonstrate the key role parables play in constructing that portrayal. Parables become, on the narrative level, indirect presentations of character traits of the

Lukan Pharisees. For example, the narrator directs the parable of the Lost Son to the Pharisees and scribes (Luke 15:3). Jesus receives tax collectors and sinners, so the Lukan Pharisees and scribes object. The three parables in Luke 15 are Jesus' entreaty to the scribes and Pharisees *as characters* to rejoice with God over the restoration of sinners. The portrait of the elder son reflects the faces of the Lukan scribes and Pharisees on the narrative level; his actions closely parallel their actions (253).[23] Until they learn to rejoice over the restoration of sinners, the parable of the Lost Son intimates that they will remain estranged from God and pitifully ignorant of God's true character (251). But Jesus still urges the Lukan scribes and Pharisees to join the celebration.

Because the primary literary contexts of parables are their locations in the Gospels, John Donahue wishes to "wed recent parable study to the results of redaction criticism of the Synoptic Gospels."[24] A major part of this book (28–193) deals with parables as texts in the literary and theological contexts of a given gospel—the only context that is directly accessible to us (4). Thus redactional interests dominate and other historical-critical issues (e.g., distinguishing between layers of tradition) at times tend to overshadow Donahue's literary analyses. Yet Donahue correctly insists that we must pay attention to the frequent, fertile, and complex interactions between parables and their immediate contexts, as well as their placement in the larger Synoptic narratives.[25]

Warren Carter and John Paul Heil in their book *Matthew's Parables*[26] focus on what happens as Matthew's audience interacts with the parables in their present form and in their current placement *within* [emphasis theirs] the plot of Matthew's gospel. Four important features mark this approach. First, Carter and Heil focus on the *final form* of the parables as they are found in Matthew. No attempt is made to reconstruct the parables as told by the historical Jesus or to examine the changes the author made to the parables. Second, they examine the parables in light of their placement in the current literary context of Matthew and do not reconstruct a possible setting in the ministry of the historical Jesus. Third, Carter and Heil pay close attention to the intratextual connections between the parables and the sections in which they are embedded but also examine their connections with the entire gospel—its plot, characters, and points of view. This reading is cumulative because they also make explicit the contribution and influence of the knowledge that the authorial audience has gained from reading the earlier sections of the gospel.[27] Finally, they do not focus on the intent of Jesus the parable teller or of the author of the gospel; they exhibit what happens as an authorial audience interacts with the parables, because an audience plays an "active role in making and living meaning" (8, 210).

These studies constructively examine the interpretive contexts the gospels themselves provide for parables, but a word of caution is in order: Tensions inevitably arise between parables and the gospel contexts in which they are embedded because no single narrative context can restrain or complete the parables' power to communicate meaning. As Bernard Brandon Scott notes, the gospels are faithful to the parables' original hermeneutical horizon, so they should be analyzed in their contexts. Yet a dialectic appears because the performances of those parables in the gospels generate inevitable "distortions" (a term he borrows from Paul Ricoeur) simply because no single performance can exhaust a narrative's potential (55–56).

As a rejoinder to Scott's position, I would argue that this relationship between gospel context and parable is not dialectic; it is *dialogic*. The point of departure for any type of study has to be the text. But once a parable is embedded into a larger narrative, its sense changes dramatically. The author's voice enters into a dialogue with the parable; the author's voice reverberates with the original utterance of the creator of the parable, *and* the narrator's voice reverberates with the utterances of the characters in the parable and other characters in the larger narrative. Yet the dialogic nature of a parable embedded in a larger narrative is also true for the "original" parable itself. Jesus' "original" utterance was, in essence, a rejoinder in an even greater dialogue, incorporating, in different ways, the words of others who had preceded him, whether from the Hebrew Bible, traditional repertoires, or elsewhere. These words were not created *ex nihilo* because this parabolic dialogue is a chain of reactions that continued in a radically new way when the historical Jesus first took the conventional language of his first-century Galilean culture and created these poetic narratives, parables that contained something absolutely new, parables that transformed what was previous.

The author of each gospel provides a rejoinder to Jesus' parables; that rejoinder may appear to claim monologic authority, but the parables of Jesus shatter that monologue. The parables still call for dialogic responses on the part of the hearers/readers. The gospel authors provided their own (canonical) responses; that is their inalienable right. But the parables, as dialogic narratives, still ask readers today to give *their* responses; that is our inalienable right and the texts' inherent demand. The one who begins to understand—or at least makes the attempt to understand—becomes a participant in that greater dialogue.[28] In essence, through our participation in that dialogue, we are "writing" our own rejoinder to the parable; we are participating in the concrete creation of "scripture."[29]

Conclusion

The advent of "fully developed" literary approaches to the parables of Jesus inaugurates a significant shift in the orientation, methodology, and language. Debates still occur about simile/metaphor, parable/allegory, and other related matters (see chapter 7 below), but implicitly or explicitly, most scholars have accepted a view of parable as primarily metaphoric in a context of which metaphoric elements actually extend to all language.[30] This development entails a shift from a primarily historical focus to a focus on the nature of language in its social, cultural, literary, historical, ideological, and rhetorical contexts. Current scholarship, as the following chapters demonstrate, is now exploring the nature of parables and the nature of language in a multitude of ways, but most of them, in varying amounts and degrees, incorporate the insights of these literary approaches—if not their orientation, methodology, and language.

4
The Parables and Their Jewish Contexts

The ever-increasing and seemingly bewildering array of recent studies on the historical Jesus reflects the diversity among scholarship—and society at large—about current perceptions of "who Jesus was."[1] The evidence is complicated because the canonical gospels present somewhat divergent portraits of Jesus, and extracanonical sources (and some "intracanonical" sources, such as the postulated "Q-Gospel")[2] present an even more complex situation. As always, the presuppositions and biases of interpreters enter into the mix—we always, inevitably and understandably, project a bit of ourselves onto our conception of the historical Jesus.[3] The parables, as an integral element of our evidence about the historical Jesus, play an important role in these reconstructions. Yet, as we have seen, basic elements concerning the parables remain in dispute. For example, should we leave the parables in their present literary contexts or examine them separately? Can we peel away, like the rind of an orange, the additions and changes made to the parables in the early churches and by the gospel authors? The difficulties of such reconstructions also exist at the most fundamental levels. Scholars, for example, even differ concerning the original language used by Jesus when he taught in parables: Aramaic, Hebrew, or Greek.[4]

A few basic facts are (almost!) without dispute: Jesus was an itinerant Jewish teacher and wonder worker who lived in Palestine during the early part of the first century C.E. Parables were part of his teaching repertoire, and to understand better their use and function as well as the creative understanding involved in their construction, we have to look at the first-century cultural contexts in which these parables were spoken and heard. The next two chapters will examine aspects of the cultural contexts that impact our understandings of the parables. Because those contexts, unlike chapters in a book, cannot be separated from one another, the overall evaluation concerning conclusions and implications must wait until the end of chapter 5.

Mashal in the Hebrew Bible

The Septuagint, the Greek translation of the Hebrew Bible from the second century B.C.E., usually translates the Hebrew word *mashal* with the Greek term *parabolē*. By its very nature, *mashal* is difficult to describe and almost impossible to define, but its "root meaning" can be seen as "to represent" or "to be like."[5] Its noun form reflects the term's fluidity because it refers to a wide range of literary forms that utilize figurative language, such as:[6]

1. *Proverbial Saying*—Most scholars agree that the proverb is the archetypal *mashal*. A proverb is popular and concrete, such as the comparison between appearances and reality found in 1 Sm 10:12: "Is Saul also among the prophets?" (cf. 1 Sm 24:13)[7] or in Ezk 18:2, which compares the actions of one generation with the results seen in the next.

2. *Byword*—These *meshalim* contain an implied comparison between present appearances (e.g., peace, prosperity) and future reality (when God's judgment will come). The "parable" is not the literary form, but it is applied directly to the people/person in trouble (or soon to be in trouble). The reference could be to

Israel as a whole (e.g., Dt 28:37; 1 Kgs 9:7), part of Israel (e.g., Jer 24:9), or to those who turn to idolatry (e.g., Ezk 14:8).

3. *Prophetic Figurative Oracle*—Primary examples of this self-descriptive category can be seen in the prophecies uttered by Balaam concerning Israel's future (e.g., Nm 23:7, 18; 24:3, 15, 20, 21, 23).[8]

4. *A Song of Derision or Taunting*—These songs describe a divine judgment that should serve as a lesson to Israel, such as the satire against the King of Babylon in Isaiah 14:4–23 or the taunt against the rich in Micah 2:4.[9]

5. *Didactic Poem*—All of the *meshalim* have a teaching function, but these instructive poems serve as historical lessons for Israel to discern the wisdom of living correctly (e.g., Jb 29; Ps 49, 78).

6. *A Wise Saying from the Elite*—These sayings, stemming from the "intellectual elite," have a riddlelike character that makes them difficult to understand. The hidden or allusive truth must be deciphered by those with the wisdom and skill to interpret it correctly (e.g., Prv 1:6; cf. Sir 39:2).

7. *Similitude and (Allegorizing) Parable*—The allegorizing parable sometimes uses imagery from nature that is narrowly interpreted as a warning lesson for the people, such as the allegory of the "Eagle and the Vine" in Ezekiel 17:3–10 or the "Boiling Pot" in Ezekiel 24:3–5. Some scholars include the book of Jonah in this category.[10]

Parable in the Hebrew Bible?

The above summary makes it quite clear that *mashal* in the Hebrew Bible covers a much broader category than the usually more limited category *parable*. *Parable* actually is a subset of the more inclusive term *mashal*, although rigid distinctions are difficult to make (Lk 4:23, for example, uses *parabolē* for the proverb, "Physician, heal thyself").

Based upon his study of the *mashal* and its relation to the *parable*, Brandon Scott offers this definition of the latter term: "A

parable is a *mashal* that employs a short narrative fiction to reference a transcendent symbol."[11] Scott thus perceives the Hebrew
Bible usage of *mashal* as "a background" against which to understand the parables of the New Testament (13), and he concludes
that *mashal* is a *genus* that is fundamentally defined by its archetype species, the proverb. Thus the Hebrew Bible uses *mashal* for
whatever is "proverblike." The *mashal*-proverb is the paradigm
of hidden or allusive truth, so all literary forms included in the
genus *mashal* have a "suppressed content"; they stand "in need of
interpretation." To put it another way, because of the *mashal's*
inherent connotative and "suggestive" language, inference and
interpretation by the reader/hearer are essential (12–13).

For Scott, the language of *mashal* is metaphorical, typically
with vivid images and concrete language. Proverbs, the *mashal's*
"archetype species," are a primary means of preserving wisdom in
an oral culture; therefore the language has to be "memorable" or
"intensive," and proverbs tend to be representative, typical, and
applied in a variety of contexts. Finally, no *mashal* in the Hebrew
Bible "directly parallels" the New Testament usage of parable as a
short narrative. We see some development toward this usage in the
Ezekiel *mashal* of the eagle and "perhaps" in Nathan's allegorical
warning to David, but Scott concludes that "parable has not yet
emerged as a genre in the Hebrew Bible" (13).[12]

Birger Gerhardsson launched a frontal assault on the idea
that narrative parables are not found in the Hebrew Bible.[13] Gerhardsson, unlike Scott, does not define *mashal.* Instead he offers a
general description of *meshalim* that includes three basic "characteristics": (1) they are brief—never whole books; (2) they are oral
or written texts—not presentations in free words; (3) they are
artistically designed—not careless colloquial speech (1988: 340;
1989: 290). Despite numerous "borderline cases" (e.g., Prv
9:1–6, 13–18; Is 28:23–29; Ezk 15:1–8; 16:1–54; 19:2–9, 10–14;
23:1–19; 24:3–14), however, Gerhardsson admits that only five
Hebrew Bible texts qualify for the designation "narrative
mashal": (1) Jotham's *mashal* of the Trees (Jgs 9:7–15); (2)

Nathan's *mashal* of the Poor Man's only Lamb (2 Sm 12:1–4); (3) Jehoash's *mashal* of the Thistle (2 Kgs 14:9); (4) Isaiah's *mashal* of the Vineyard (Is 5:1–6); (5) Ezekiel's *mashal* of the Vine and the Eagles (Ezk 17:3–10).[14] The list narrows, however, because numbers 1, 3, and 5 are fables and number 4 is an allegorizing parable. Gerhardsson is left with only Nathan's "narrative parable" as the type often found in the Synoptic Gospels, and, in a somewhat polemical way, Gerhardsson also stresses the significant differences between the *meshalim* in the Hebrew Bible and the "narrative *meshalim*" in the New Testament (1988:348–54), thus undercutting, to a certain extent, his main argument.[15]

Mashal in Recent Research

Other investigations, however, have brought the discussion concerning the *mashal* closer to the discussion of "parable." In doing so, they highlight the performative and decision-making quality inherent in the *mashal* itself.[16]

George Landes sees the didactic function of the *mashal* primarily as a moral lesson to be learned and, of course, acted on (see note 10 above). Landes generally deals with matters of content and function because he feels that those elements, more than form (i.e., pattern or structure), determined whether or not something was a *mashal* (139). David Suter, however, argues that Landes had paid insufficient attention to matters of form in the *mashal*.[17] Therefore, despite the diversity of form, content, and function in the *meshalim,* Suter postulates a set of "family resemblances" between various examples of *meshalim.* The family resemblances became the model itself by employing a complex set of comparisons and contrasts (e.g., between the fate of the righteous and the wicked in the present and future). In addition, in the Similitudes of Enoch (1 Enoch 37–71; Jewish work[s] roughly contemporaneous with the beginning of the Christian era), the concept of *mashal* connects eschatological and cosmological elements—which, as seen in chapter 7 below, is a matter still under discussion in scholarship about the parables of Jesus.

Timothy Polk applauded the advances made by Landes and Suter, particularly their clear use of the term *genre* and their recognition that *mashal* did not have a fixed literary form, but instead could be applied to a variety of literary types.[18] Polk feels that previous discussions, however, ignored the "heightened performative and reader-involving quality"—what he calls the "noetic function" of these "speech acts" (569)—that make them particularly suitable for religious discourse (564). Polk sees the *mashal* in Ezekiel, for example, as reader involving and behavior affecting; it "involves its addressee, or target, in self-judgment" (570).

As Lawrence Boadt notes, these studies show a number of points of agreement. All agree that *mashal* is not a set literary form per se but a general concept that has a wide range of forms. All agree that the *mashal* has a didactic function, portrays a "norm," and asks the reader/hearer to respond appropriately. In addition, one finds a common trajectory: all move the discussion of the *mashal* closer to the discussion of *parable* in current rabbinic and New Testament scholarship, which is clearly seen in their greater willingness to refer to *mashal* as *parable* (176).

The Parable as *Mashal:* The Case of Rabbinic Literature

Unfortunately, scholarship concerning the *mashal* has, over the years, been plagued by polemical discourse. Christian scholars tend to disparage the *meshalim* in rabbinic literature, for example, and Jewish scholars tend to react defensively to refute such charges.[19] Israel Abrahams, in his work *Studies in Pharisaism and the Gospels,*[20] spends a chapter disputing the "inferiority" of rabbinic parables. He argues that there probably was no systematic dependence in either direction and agrees with previous scholars who posited that Jesus' parables fit comfortably within an already-established Jewish tradition. A few years later, Asher Feldman, in his book, *The Parables and Similes of the Rabbis,*[21] similarly has to "justify," in a polemical way, the literary and artistic merits of the rabbinic *meshalim.*

These two books also have to be seen within the framework of (New Testament) parable scholarship's massive "continental divide": before and after Adolph Jülicher. Christian scholars, such as Christian Bugge, utilized the *mashal* to refute Jülicher's "Aristotelian" view of parables. Bugge argues, against Jülicher, that the Jewish *mashal* included allegorical elements and that Jesus' parables arose in this Jewish context. Paul Fiebig's works on the parables take Bugge's work as their starting point but includes a much more extensive analysis. Fiebig's first book incorporates an analysis of similes, parables, and allegorical sayings from the *Mekilta,* a midrashic commentary on part of Exodus, which he compares to the parables of Jesus. Fiebig discovers great similarities, such as the presentation of the background, occasion, opening formulas, and explanations, as well as some slight resemblances in content.[22] Fiebig's somewhat neglected work is seriously flawed by its polemical tone and agenda—he stresses, for example, the "superiority" and "lack of trivialness" of the parables of Jesus in comparison to the parables of the *Mekilta.* Yet his emphasis on the importance of oral traditions, the necessity of understanding the Hebraic context of the *mashal,* and the similarities between the style, expression, and modes of thought in the Synoptic parables with the extant *meshalim* were significant contributions to our understanding of the parables of Jesus.[23]

Because of the still unresolved questions and the deficiencies in previous research on rabbinic parables (such as the concentration on midrash or the shadow of Christian or Jewish presuppositions), recent scholars have attempted more complete and less ideologically driven investigations of the rabbinic parables.[24] In a 1989 essay, for example, Clemens Thoma defines *rabbinic parables* as "simple, secular, mono-episodic, fictional narrative units that serve to explain the rabbinic understanding of the Torah."[25] The rabbis used these rhetorical and argumentative forms for preaching, to defend their identity, and to provide guidance in their audiences' daily lives. All rabbinic parables have a twofold structure: the narrative proper *(mashal)* and normative instruction *(nimshal)*. Although this structural analysis is limited to two parts, Thoma postulates five major "elements" involved in the communicative process of almost all rabbinic parables (27–31):

1. *Motivation*—The motivation is the situation that has to be addressed, clarified, or answered. It could be a discussion among rabbinic scholars or the need for an apologetic clarification. This situation induced the creation of a metaphoric parable to provide insight into the Torah, as understood by the parable's creator(s).

2. *Hiddush*—The second part of the introduction is the *Hiddush,* the creative idea of the *mashal* teller, which makes clear the narrator-writer's religious strategy for making the light of the Torah shine for a new audience. This "primary point of disclosure" includes a "hinge phrase" or aspect on which the primary comparison will be made with the *mashal.*[26]

3. *Mashal*—The *mashal* proper is an ordinary narrative account with a simple plot. The simple dramatic episode, though referential, is not just a comparison, and it stems from the creative imagination of its creator. An important element is that the *mashal* is composed (or possibly modified from an existing story) "to fit into the normative preaching of the *nimshal*" (30).

4. *Nimshal*—The *nimshal* is the explanation of the *mashal,* and there is always a strong connection between the *nimshal* and the motivation of the parable. The *nimshal* can be introduced by the formulaic "so" or "in a similar way," and it consists of biblical quotations and rabbinical expressions that are intended to give an authoritative explanation of the Torah.

5. *The Addressees*—The intention of the parable is to influence the community; therefore the addressees include the entire community, not just one individual, and the addressees may include future Jewish generations.

Although Thoma does not compare his tentative conclusions with the parables of the Jesus tradition, a few of his conclusions have direct relevance: He argues that the rabbinic parables appear to be the "best representatives of rabbinic theology" (37), which, if true, may give some credence to the assumption that the parables of Jesus portray major, essential elements of his teaching. Thoma also notes that the importance of the rabbinic parables is made clear by their simplicity, clarity, and the great conscientiousness of composition. This composition proclaims the presence of God with Israel, which, as always, has a clear ethical dimension—including the responsibility of the whole community to have an attitude of repentance (38–39). Finally, Thoma observes that many rabbinic parables deal with Israel's salvation history and have eschatological aims. Thus these parables provide another important point of comparison with the parables of Jesus and his proclamation of the kingdom of God as found in the Synoptic Gospels.

Thoma's five "descriptive elements" do not, however, convey all the explicit structural characteristics found in most rabbinic parables. This task, in a midrashic context, was more fully undertaken by Harvey K. McArthur and Robert M. Johnston in their book *They Also Taught in Parables*. They assert that the immediate environment and internal structure of the narrative *mashal* in "its fullest narrative form" (i.e., frequently one or more elements is lacking) include five parts. I will define the various parts and then illustrate those parts with a rabbinic parable from *Deuteronomy Rabbah* (Dt R. 2:24):[27]

1. *Illustrand*—the matter to be illustrated, proved, or explained. It is not directly a part of the parable structurally, but it provides the immediate context and, in fact, the reason for its placement/existence. Most rabbinic parables have an explicit illustrand:

> "Another explanation [of] 'Thou wilt return to the Lord thy God'" (Dt 4:30).

2. *Introductory Formula*—the preparatory prefix to the story. There are many variations, but all serve the same purpose. A tripartite formula is common, such as: (a) "I will parable you a parable"; (b) "Unto what is the matter like?"; (c) "It is like a king who…":

> "R. [i.e., Rabbi] Samuel Pargrita said in the name of R. Meir: Unto what is the matter like? It is like the son of a king who took to evil ways.…"

3. *Parable Proper*—the illustrative story. Common examples are parables involving stories about kings, fables (with animals), or wisdom parables:

> "It is like the son of a king who took to evil ways. The king sent a tutor to him who appealed to him, saying: Repent my son. But the son sent him back to his father [with a message], How can I have the effrontery to return? I am ashamed to come before you. Thereupon his father sent back word: My son, is a son ever ashamed to return to his father? And is it not to your father that you will be returning?"

4. *Application*—the great majority of rabbinic parables attach an explicit interpretation or application, which makes "the" point quite clear. The application is often introduced by the word *kak* (even so, or likewise):

> "Even so the Holy One, blessed be He, sent Jeremiah to Israel when they sinned, and said to him: Go, say to my children: Return."

5. *Scriptural Quotation*—often introduced by the formula "as it is said" or "as it is written," to which one or more scriptural quotations intended to "clinch the point" could be appended. The quotation is often followed by another application, which then could become an *illustrand* itself, thus producing another parable, and so forth (99–125). The following example intermingles scriptural quotations with additional applications:

"Whence this? For it is said: 'Go, and proclaim these words' etc. (Jer 3:12). Israel asked Jeremiah: How can we have the effrontery to return to God? Whence do we know this? For it is said: 'Let us lie down in our shame and let our confusion cover us' etc. (3:25). But God sent back word to them: My children, if you return, will you not be returning to your Father? Whence this? 'For I am become a father to Israel' etc. (Jer 31:9)"

To this point, however, there appear to be striking dissimilarities between rabbinic parables and the parables of Jesus, both in form and content. The most common arguments for distancing the parables of Jesus from the rabbinic parables are easily cited. First, among the extant evidence—even though dating of precise elements is problematic—the parables in the Synoptics predate the parables in rabbinic literature. Second, the form of all of these stories seems to have changed over time, with various usage, and in various contexts. The rabbinic parables, whatever their initial usage, primarily serve as a rhetorical device for exegesis. As such, the rabbinic parables assume a much more standardized form and more stereotypical features, a change that tends to become more pronounced over time. In addition, the rabbinic parables tend to exceed the Synoptic parables in the degree of their explicit interpretation. Finally, many (Christian) scholars argue that rabbinic parables—in contrast to many parables of Jesus—tend to reinforce the conventional wisdom or the societal norms of various rabbis and the community.[28] I hesitate to endorse this last argument for two basic reasons: (a) some rabbinic parables appear to critique society in a way comparable to many social critiques in Jesus' parables; (b) in their present contexts, the Synoptic parables are well on their way to being "domesticated." By that I mean the parables of Jesus, *as utilized in the gospels,* begin to reinforce the "conventional wisdom" or the "societal norms" of the early Christian communities.

Rabbinic Parables and the Parables of Jesus

Other scholars, such as David Flusser, have investigated the *mashal* and have found an identifiable trajectory that leads them to conclude that the similarities between rabbinic parables and the Synoptic parables are much more striking than the dissimilarities.

Flusser believes that Jesus' primary language was Hebrew, although it was possible that Jesus also spoke Aramaic "from time to time."[29] Flusser argues that New Testament parables and rabbinic parables share compositional similarities. These similarities include such items as formulaic elements of diction, conventional themes, and stereotyped motifs, all of which indicate that both rabbinic parables and the parables of Jesus stem from a common narrative tradition. This common tradition has affinities with the fables of Aesop, so Flusser suggests that the antecedents *("Gattung")* of the Jewish parables could be found in Greek philosophy.[30] The parables themselves, however, were a development within Palestine. The differences between Jesus' parables and rabbinic parables, Flusser argues, could be explained by the fact that the parables of Jesus belong to an older type of rabbinic parable, a nonexegetical "ethical" type (he also postulates an intermediate form, a parabolic proverb, which he sees reflected in Mt 9:37–38). The differences between Jesus' parables and rabbinic parables were primarily due to a changing of focus: the explanation of biblical passages.

Flusser's interesting, but speculative, reconstruction formed the foundation for the work done by his student, Brad Young.[31] Young seems particularly concerned to lessen the distance between rabbinic parables and the parables of Jesus. So an important foundation of Young's study is his acceptance of Flusser's thesis that the two traditions actually are the same, unique genre that serves to elucidate and/or illustrate teaching (e.g., 236). Jesus was one of the "outstanding Parabolists" of his day, one who stood firmly within the (same) Jewish tradition (180). Some of Jesus' parables are not only similar in theme and form to rabbinic parables, but they contain similar illustrative motifs and examples, and they have a continuity of expression. Thus they stand in a common stream of the rabbinical world of instruction (37). To corroborate his thesis, Young also seeks to demonstrate that Jesus, like the later rabbis, originally told his parables in Hebrew. Young even translates some of the parables from Greek into Hebrew, but the result is extremely unconvincing.

Philip Culbertson realizes that Hebrew or Aramiac source documents for the Greek texts of the gospels may not have ever existed, but he insists that Jesus' parables "are conditioned by the Arameo-Hebraic religion and culture out of which they proceed and thus cannot be forced into Greek categories of mentation."[32] Culbertson believes that because oral tradition would have kept stock figures and associations alive for several generations, rabbinic parables may shed important light on the parables of Jesus (19–20). The parables of Jesus, he suggests, can be seen as "halakhic midrash."[33]

David Stern provides us with the most sophisticated methodological approach to the midrashic rabbinic parables to date.[34] Stern gathers data to suggest that the rabbis initially used parables in a variety of contexts—including recitations at banquets, as responses to polemical questions and challenges, or a means of expression during a time of public crisis. The most common uses, however, were the delivery of the sermon in the synagogue and the study of the Torah in the academy. In fact, the rabbis became convinced that the parable form itself was created for this latter usage (1986:632–33).

Citing three different approaches to the parables taken by New Testament scholars, Stern attempts to steer the middle course through the two more exclusivistic approaches. The first approach sees the *mashal* as primarily a didactic instrument, where the abstract is made concrete; that is, a difficult concept is made easier to understand and therefore would be immediately understood by the (original) audience. Later audiences would not know the immediate context, so the *nimshal* was created later to clarify what was originally quite clear. The second approach, Stern argues, views the *mashal* as an oblique or even secret way of speaking to the "initiated"; hence the *mashal* is seen as primarily allegorical. A few texts supporting both these views can be found in rabbinical literature, but the third approach best explains the evidence: The *mashal* is "an allusive narrative told for an ulterior purpose," whose "purpose" can usually be defined as praise or blame of a specific situation of the author and audience of this fictional narrative.

In other words, the *mashal* draws a series of parallels between the story recounted in the narrative and the "actual situation" to which the *mashal* is directed. These parallels, however, are not drawn explicitly; the audience is left to derive them for themselves. So the *mashal* is not a simple tale with a transparent lesson nor a completely opaque story with a secret message; the *mashal* is a narrative that actively elicits from its audience the application of its message (i.e., the interpretation).

The social context, then, clarifies the "message" of the *mashal* by giving the audience all the information they need. Here Stern's approach encounters several problems: First, most *meshalim* in rabbinic literature are preserved not in narrative contexts, but exegetical ones (i.e., in the study of scripture), and there seems to be no important formal or functional differences between *meshalim* embedded in other narratives and those presented in exegetical contexts (1991:7); in both, the rabbis used them as rhetorical devices. In fact, once the *mashal* was embedded into any literary context, Stern admits, the "real context" was no longer immediately present or available. In an attempt to clarify "the original context" (1986:637), the *nimshal* was provided. In a later work Stern clarifies his position concerning the "original context" by stating that the *nimshal* provides the "secondhand audience" with the necessary information it needs to understand the *mashal's* message (1989:45–48, 59, 72). At best, the narrative will present a secondhand account of what that "reality" was. As the context changes—in form and audience—a parable's meaning will also change, and it will change even more when a parable's medium is shifted from oral to literary (1991:17–18).

Stern agrees that it is difficult to trace the "lineage" of parabolic narratives that have human characters in ancient Near Eastern literature: The earliest full-fledged fictional narratives are found in the Hebrew Bible (e.g., 2 Sm 12:1–14), but these parables seem to be used as legal strategms (1991:186). Few parables are found in postbiblical literature (e.g., 4 Esdras 4:13). Yet parables and fables are very much at home in "traditional cultures" that still utilize oral traditions, as evidenced best, perhaps, by a literary form found in the ancient Greek epic: the *ainos,* a genre that includes fables and tales (1991:6).

Even so, Stern disagrees with Flusser's contention that this literary form was imported from Hellenistic sources, such as popular Greco-Roman philosophy. Stern concludes that the scarcity of extant examples of parables from around the time of the Christian era may be due to the fact that it was a popular, *oral* form of address utilized in teaching and preaching (1991:187).

Stern's work, in spite of these differences from Flusser's conclusions, thus led him to agree with Flusser's main argument that the parables of Jesus and rabbinic parables share a common background and compositional similarities: The parables of Jesus are our earliest datable evidence "for the tradition of the *mashal* that attains its full maturity in Rabbinic literature" (1989:43),[35] where the *mashal* assumed its "normative, standard form" (1991:7). Because the rabbinic parables are the closest evidence for the literary form of parable as Jesus may have used it, they offer valuable, unique evidence for how a common literary tradition has been directed to different ends.

In their present literary forms as ideological narratives, parables are constructed by design and rhetoric to impress a certain world view upon their audiences. Stern attempts to ascertain how these ideological narratives perform that function. He argues that through the refusal to state its message directly, the *mashal* actually becomes more effective in persuading the audience of its essential truth: It deliberately gives the impression of naming its meaning "insufficiently" (1991:15). Thus the *mashal* artfully manipulates its audience to become actively involved to "deduce" meaning from the two "enactments" of that message (i.e., the *mashal* and the *nimshal*).[36]

To sum up, Stern concludes that the Jesus of the Synoptic Gospels utilized *parable* in essentially the same way as the rabbis employed the *mashal*—in public contexts (e.g., preaching) and as an instrument for praise and blame, often directed at persons present in his audience. Jesus' parables, like the rabbis' parables, were exoteric—their messages could have been comprehended by their original audiences without much difficulty (*pace* Mk 4:11–12). Stern, however, tends to overstress the similarities—and downplay the differences—between Synoptic and rabbinic parables. This tendency results in certain overgeneralizations, such as his "discovery" of some equivalent to the rigorous rabbinic *nimshal* in New Testament parables.[37] He also tends to overlook the radical role of reversal and societal critique as portrayed in the parables of Jesus, although comparable critiques may be found in some rabbinic parables as well.

These caveats notwithstanding, Sterns's works are a significant contribution that advances our insight into the methodological, ideological, and historical problems involved in parable study, as well as our understanding of the rabbinic parables themselves.

5
The Parables and Their Hellenistic Contexts

Although Jesus was a first-century Jewish teacher and wonder worker, the parables, in their present contexts, are in Greek. The Jewish heritage of the Jesus portrayed in the Synoptic Gospels—who teaches in parables—merges with Hellenistic-Roman forms of speech, thought, and action, so that the "Synoptic Jesus" speaks and acts in roles that combine Jewish and Hellenistic-Roman modes of words and deeds.[1] Because Hellenistic culture influenced all Diaspora Judaism and Palestinian Judaism to a certain extent, the Jewishness of the Synoptic Jesus does not preclude the existence of Hellenistic elements. A careful reading makes clear that the gospels merge biblical patterns with Hellenistic patterns and conventions; they—and the Jesus they portray—are intercultural.

The Greek Language of the Parables

Robert Funk stated, with only a hint of equivocation, that "the language of the parables almost certainly took shape in Greek" because the textures of the parables give the impression that they were originally heard in Greek and composed by a competent, native speaker of Greek.[2] Funk discovers, for example, the ancient

Greek emphasis of assonance in composition (i.e., the recurrence of a sound in such a manner as to catch the ear) in the narrative parables *in Greek,* which raised questions about the language in which Jesus composed them. Funk acknowledges that Matthew Black, for one (in his *An Aramaic Approach to the Gospels*), found many examples of alliteration, assonance (repetition of similar vowel sounds), and paronomasia after he translated portions of the New Testament back into Aramaic, but Funk argues that this only indicated the importance of such euphony in the "common languages of Hellenistic-Roman Palestine" (1977:48).[3]

What interests Funk is that provocative forms of assonance exist in the parables in Greek, enough for him to claim that "the major narrative parables provide ample evidence of having been composed in Greek" (1977:49). The Greek of the parables was not translated from Aramaic. Instead it is "vacuumed Greek"—an unadorned form of Greek marked by its simplicity in style and diction. This style of Greek, Funk argues, would come from someone unversed in more complicated Greek, someone whose primary language may have been Aramaic.[4]

Funk's arguments have not won many converts,[5] but Charles Hedrick's work seems to verify, at least in part, Funk's arguments about the importance of euphony in the parables in Greek.[6] Hedrick stresses the need for being sensitive to the "rhythm of the narrative," which includes aspects of "sound devices" such as alliteration, assonance, consonance (repetition of similar consonantal sounds), and onomatopoeia (60–61). Hedrick does not interact directly with Funk's conclusion that the parables were initially spoken in Greek, however. Instead he notes that the form in which one analyzes the poetics of the parables will not be the language or the form of their "original audition."[7] So Hedrick's investigation of euphony may give little information about the "initial" form of the parables, but it does reveal much about their present characteristics in early Christian literature (61). In fact, one of Hedrick's primary contributions is his innovative work on recognizing the critical nature of *sound* in both the structure of the parables and in the way the stories are organized.

The Parables and Greek Fables

Adolph Jülicher noted that "the majority of the *parabolai* of Jesus, the ones bearing a narrative form, are fables, such as the ones of Stesichoros and of Aesop."[8] Jülicher's judgment, needless to say, has not gained wide acceptance. Most parable scholars ignore such comparisons. When a scholar does raise the issue of Greek fables, they are usually dismissed with a distinction between parable and fable such as the one used by T. W. Manson: *parable* tends to depict human relations by inventing cases analogous to what happens in real life. *Fable,* on the other hand, is "pure fiction," which often invests animals, birds, and plants with human attributes.[9] Madeline Boucher echoes Manson's sentiments, but she includes the judgment that fables have a "prudential lesson," whereas parables have a "religious or moral lesson" which is "typically Semitic."[10]

In antiquity the term *fable* denotes several kinds of brief narratives, including those that directly stem from human experience. Aelius Theon, for example, defined *fable* more generally as "a fictitious story picturing a truth," a definition enthusiastically endorsed by the classicist Ben Edwin Perry.[11] In fact, many fables are about humans and the gods; thus they can convey religious truths (xxiv). In contrast to David Flusser's claim that the *mashal* was dependent upon the Greek environment (e.g., Greek philosophy, Aesop's fables), Perry argues the reverse: The Greek fable had its literary-historical roots in the Semitic East. In fact, Perry claims, the Hebrew *mashal* is the *precursor* of the Aesopic fable.[12]

In her article, "Parable and Fable," Mary Ann Beavis accepts Perry's judgment and argues that ancient Near Eastern stories were the prototypes of both Greek fables and Jewish parables (478). The affinities between the two are thus traceable to their common origins. Beavis illustrates these affinities by selecting several

Greek fables and describing five basic similarities between these fables and narrative parables:

1. *Similarities in narrative structure*—Fables and parables are brief, invented narratives that shed light on aspects of human experience and behavior.

2. *Similarities in content*—Fables are not fantastic stories but involve ordinary human characters and situations, such quarreling siblings who are corrected by a loving father. Yet despite their realism, these fables also contain an element of extravagance.

3. *Religious and ethical themes*—Beavis then focuses on two Greek fables to illustrate the relations between humans and the gods, but the religious and moral tones of the fables make clear the differences between the religious and ethical traditions. In fact, only two of Jesus' parables have direct supernatural interventions (Lk 12:13–21; 16:19–31).

4. *An element of surprise or irony*—Both of the above fables have an element of reversal that is reminiscent of Jesus' parables.

5. *Secondary morals or application*—Most of the fables Beavis examines have morals, either attached to the beginning or the end of the fable. These morals appear to be secondary, however; they do not necessarily fit the stories very well. Both Matthew and Luke tend to add such moralizing features either to the beginning of a parable (e.g., Lk 18:1) or at the end (e.g., Mt 18:32–33; 20:13–15).

Beavis's article is inherently a plea to broaden the avenues presently under discussion. She appropriately questions the presupposition of many New Testament scholars that the Hebrew Bible and rabbinic *meshalim* are the *only* appropriate comparative material we have for examining the literary and cultural milieus of the Synoptic parables. Her claim that the fable was used in elementary exercises in Greek composition taught in schools all over the

Roman Empire makes her overall scenario more plausible: School children learned composition by hearing, reciting, and writing down in their own words fables that were read or told to them (477). Beavis argues, citing Funk's conclusion about the parables being composed in Greek, that it is indeed possible that Jesus was directly or indirectly influenced by such popular Hellenistic-Roman popular literature as the Greek fable. In addition, the Synoptic authors most certainly had at least a Greek elementary education and might well have (further?) shaped the parables into the literary class of fable (494). If that is indeed the case, the rhetorical function of such composition deserves further exploration.

The Parables and *Paideia*[13]

Many New Testament scholars are casting their comparative nets in areas beyond the Jewish cultural waters; they are discovering in the broader range of Hellenistic-Roman literature and culture many aspects that expand dramatically our understanding of the first-century contexts in which the parables were spoken/written and heard/read. Ronald Hock, for example, has pointed to the limitations of current scholarship's investigations of the parable of the Rich Man and Lazarus (Lk 16:19–31). He has persuasively called for a broader comparative framework for reading the parable, one that includes various rhetorical, literary, and philosophical texts from the Hellenistic-Roman intellectual tradition.[14] Specifically Hock sees a close congruence of this parable with Cynic views on wealth and poverty (448).

Hock argues that the repeated claims that the parable of Lazarus and the Rich Man was adapted from an ancient Egyptian folktale are overstated—the "parallels…are neither compelling nor as explanatory" as suggested in scholarship. He laments the fact that sources from the larger Hellenistic-Roman environment are seldom considered seriously as comparative texts,[15] and he argues that the parable of the Rich Man and Lazarus in particular "has an unmistakable Cynic coloring" (462). To demonstrate his thesis, Hock cites the Lucian texts *Gallus* and *Cataplus,* in which the poor man Micyllus is compared with rich men. Micyllus, a poor, marginalized artisan, goes hungry from early morning to evening, and he must bear the slights, insults, and beatings of the powerful. At their deaths, Micyllus and the rich tyrant Megapenthes make the trip to Hades. Megapenthes, like the rich man in Jesus' parable, tries to strike a bargain to alter his situation, but to no avail. Finally, Micyllus and Megapenthes face Rhadamanthus, the judge of the underworld. Micyllus is judged to be pure and goes to the Isles of the Blessed. Megapenthes's soul, however, is stained with corruption, and he will be appropriately punished (459–60). In Hock's opinion, both this story and the parable of the Rich Man and Lazarus betray Cynic views on wealth and poverty (463).

Hock argues that many elements of these two parables, such as the reversal in the fortunes of the characters after death, partake in the broader arena of the social and intellectual life of traditional Mediterranean society (461). By limiting the comparative texts *only* to Jewish contexts, scholars place artificial blinders on their eyes, blinders that hinder access to the cultures in which this parable might have arisen and been told in the first century, and certainly in which it would have been heard.[16]

F. G. Downing, in his book *Cynics and Christian Origins,* corroborates Hock's conclusions. Downing argues that although figurative speech occurs in many ancient sources, it was the Cynics who particularly follow the example of Socrates by frequently using illustrations, especially those drawn from "ordinary life."[17] The correspondence with the Jesus tradition recorded in the Q Gospel is substantial, both in general (the sheer quantity of parable, metaphor, and simile) and in particular (in specific references).[18] Downing asserts that the style of Jesus' teaching displays a distinctive combination of Cynicism and Judaism, which presupposes a Cynic-influenced Galilean Jewish culture (157). In addition, since Jesus' parables are an open invitation for his hearers that disturb their perceptions and unsettle their acceptance of what they take for granted, the only close analogies in ancient literature are the Cynics' use of figurative language that attempted to subvert cultural norms (157–58).

Other scholars have provided examples from an even broader spectrum of Hellenistic-Roman culture. For example, the rather puzzling presentation of Jesus' parables in Mark 4:1–34 (especially 11–12, 33–34) has proved to be fruitful soil for much scholarly speculation, both with and without "depth of root." Burton Mack's analysis is one controversial entry into this discussion,[19] but one that illustrates the fertile nature of various comparative texts from Hellenistic-Roman traditions.

Mack acknowledges that the images of field, sowing, seeds, and harvest are standard metaphors in Jewish apocalyptic, wisdom, and prophetic traditions for God's dealings with Israel. Mack, however, contends that this precise usage of such traditions would be conceivable for a later Christian thinker, but not for the historical Jesus (1988:55).

To cite just one example: The content of the parable of the Seeds makes one "suspicious," because agricultural images, especially that of sowing seed, were standard analogies for *paideia* during this era. First-century Mediterranean ears would have heard this analogy/parable and "would have immediately recalled the stock image" for instruction, especially that of inculcating Hellenistic culture![20] These stock analogies utilized the sower (teacher) who sowed (taught) his seed (words) upon various soils (students). Therefore, this parable in Mark that illustrates Jesus' "mysterious" teaching (4:11) actually was itself an established image of instruction. Because the imagery and the standard mode of referencing in the parable would have been quite clear to most first-century persons, the "mystery" has to reside in the nature of the culture and/or kingdom the parable seeks to illustrate (1988:160). Mack then attempts to show how the entire section (4:1–34) constructs a cogent and clever rhetorical elaboration of the parable of the Seeds—one that follows conventional modes of argumentation (1988:162–65).

Vernon K. Robbins provides an analysis of Mack's study that demonstrates what relationship this "parable rhetoric" in Mark 4 had with both "Jewish culture" and "Hellenistic-Roman culture."[21] Robbins argues that the ultimate goal of "parable rhetoric" in Mark 4 was to ask—and, for some, to answer—the question: "How can a person receive the Kingdom of God and become fruitful?" (74). In social terms, this type of rhetoric is "manipulationist" because it seeks a transformed set of relationships (61). The social rhetoric of Mark 4 interacts with both Jewish culture and Hellenistic-Roman culture, and this interaction is twofold: On one hand, the argumentation is "deeply embedded" in Jewish *and* Hellenistic-Roman modes of culture, for example, by assuming many elements of those cultures; on the other hand, in this complex and variegated relationship, the parables in Mark 4 also reject, subvert, or transform other features found in Jewish and in Hellenistic-Roman cultures (80–81).

Willi Braun's study of the parable of the Great Dinner in Luke 14:16–24 also exhibits the productive nature of Hellenistic-Roman comparative texts and demonstrates very well the variegated interaction it has with its social, cultural, and literary environments.[22] This parable itself is set within a crucial meal scene in Luke's Gospel. The healing of the man with dropsy is the fourth and final Sabbath healing performed by Jesus in Luke, and it takes place during the third and final meal that Jesus shares in a Pharisee's house.[23]

In Luke 14:1–14, Jesus chastises (again) the social elite for seeking after honor. The narrator explains that Jesus observed how the guests scrambled for "places of honor" (14:7). Thus the narrative, as it has done repeatedly, closely identifies the Lukan Pharisees with the desire for self-glorification. The narrative intimately connects such self-aggrandizement to a love of possessions and a disregard for the poor, as Jesus' words and parable illustrate (14:7–24).

Braun's investigation of Hellenistic-Roman texts brings to light an element of the narrative that modern readers had previously not recognized. The man with dropsy makes a critical contribution to the narrative's rhetorical argument in this setting. Dropsy is a metaphor used by the Cynics because of the paradoxical symptoms of dropsy: The person suffering from dropsy has an unquenchable craving for fluids, even though the body is already inflated with fluid, and when the person drinks more fluids, it serves not to ease but to advance the dropsy. The symbolism is abundantly clear to readers familiar with this first-century metaphor: At a meal scene with the social elite, the man with dropsy symbolizes the rapacious and avaricious persons whom Jesus denounces in Braun's words, "with a barrage of terms that reads like a Hellenistic thesaurus of slurs" (69).

Utilizing Hellenistic-Roman comparative literature, Braun also clarifies disputed items in the interpretation of the parable itself. He decisively demonstrates, for example, that all three of the guests' excuses for rejecting the host's final summons are rooted in the guests' "single, compelling interest in the acquisition of property" (137). Even the third excuse, the acquisition of a wife, is viewed by social elite as a property transfer and/or the means of generating a legitimate son as an heir to ensure that property remained in the family. This abiding concern for material goods not only corresponds to one of Luke's central themes, but when the invited guests are seen in this light, it also has a significant impact on interpretations of the parable.

Also, in first-century cultural terms, the host's dinner invitation is a ceremonial replication of his commitment to the values of aristocratic culture. His invitation to persons of his own social standing was a central means of preserving (or enhancing) his pride of place in society. The surprising about-face of the guests who refuse the host's final summons to dinner—after previously accepting the initial invitation—is a glaring example of peer exclusion, a punitive measure of disentitlement and disaffiliation with the intention of inflicting harm upon the host (209).[24]

Previous interpretations of the parable had speculated about whether the invited guests "symbolized" the Jews and which group that was "compelled" to come symbolized the Gentiles—those interpretations reflect the version of the parable in the greater literary context of Luke's Gospel. With his use of Hellenistic-Roman texts, however, Braun constructs an extremely plausible hypothesis: The parable is a rejection of all types of self-aggrandizement, love of money, love of honor and prestige, and a radical statement of an egalitarianism that rejects the social and economic mores of the elite.

Conclusion

The exploration of Jesus' parables in conjunction with comparative texts from both Jewish and Hellenistic-Roman narratives is not merely an exercise in literary and historical "priority" or "superiority." Instead what we can learn is that the parables of Jesus were not told in a literary, cultural, social, and historical vacuum. The parables were created and preserved in conversations with their cultural environments, and they partake, vigorously at times, in that dialogical social discourse.

The early Christian era, in fact the entire Hellenistic era, was an age of active polyglossia, that is, a time when different national languages were interacting within the same cultural systems. Scattered throughout the entire Mediterranean were cities, settlements, and other areas where several cultures and languages directly "cohabited," and they interwove with each other in distinctive patterns.[25] Parables thus germinated and flourished in these fields of active polyglossia because parables themselves are dialogues that actively engage a wide range of different cultures, societies, and peoples.

Future analyses of the parables also should continue to explore other ancient narratives, both Jewish and Hellenistic-Roman—including such items as the *mashal,* parable, and fable—to learn more about first-century literary and cultural conventions in the Synoptic parables and how they interact among and with each other in various first-century contexts. If we want to continue our own dialogues with the parables, we have to become more aware of the numerous and diverse webs of signification in these narratives. Only such an open and interdisciplinary approach can facilitate the dialogue which these texts themselves inherently request.

6
The Parables and Their Social Contexts

One of the most fruitful developments in New Testament scholarship is the emergence of studies concerning the social and cultural contexts of the first-century Mediterranean world.[1] Many social and cultural elements found in ancient literature are not usually self-evident to modern readers, so aspects of the parables are virtually incomprehensible without an understanding of the social and cultural processes which influence these texts. The aim of this chapter, then, is to explore some of the significant social elements reflected in these parables.

Parables and the Social Sciences

In 1976 Kenneth Bailey noted that despite numerous scholarly investigations of the parables, the "cultural milieu" still needed serious attention.[2] To overcome the "cultural foreignness" between modern readers and first-century Palestine, Bailey proposes an "Oriental exegesis" (29–43) that combines standard critical tools of "Western scholarship" with cultural insights gained from ancient literature, contemporary peasants, and Oriental versions (Syriac and Arabic) of the New Testament (30, 36).[3]

This approach and ones similar to it provide an abundance of useful information and enrich our insights of first-century

Palestine, but the gain in information is at times offset by the lack of theoretical models for analyzing, evaluating, and processing data.[4] How can we assess, for example, whether selected data is implicit in these texts or whether we are imposing another interpretive matrix on them? Bailey's eclectic, inductive approach does not clarify or make explicit a guiding theoretical structure, so his readers do not have the opportunity to see clearly all of the implications, limitations, and biases inherent in his agenda.[5]

Bernard Brandon Scott provides a more explicit approach.[6] He schematically organizes the parables around three basic elements of first-century life ("Family, Village, City, and Beyond," "Masters and Servants," and "Home and Farm")[7] because Mediterranean and Jewish culture employed these aspects to represent symbolically its organization of the sacred. Jesus' parables utilize these patterns and "most often play against them" (74), so it is critical to understand this social-world perspective if we are to understand Jesus' parables even at the most basic literary level.

William Herzog's *Parables as Subversive Speech* provides the most explicit and detailed analysis of the social setting of the parables. In contrast to Scott's work, Herzog's approach does not subordinate social analysis to literary analysis. In fact, Herzog claims that the differences between the "Dodd-Jeremias" historical-critical tradition (see chapter 1 above) and the literary-critical tradition (see chapters 2 and 3 above) were minimal. Both produced "idealist" readings of the parables and generated a discourse that was finally unrelated to the material details of its story world (13).

The crucial difference in Herzog's approach is that he views the parables through the lens of a "pedagogy of the oppressed."[8] The focus of the parables, Herzog argues, is not on a vision of the glory of the reign (kingdom) of God, but on the gory details of how oppression serves the interests of a ruling class. Parables explore how human beings could respond to break the spiral of violence and the cycle of poverty created by such exploitation. Therefore the parables of Jesus were forms of social analysis just as much as they were forms of theological reflection (3).

Honor and Shame

One of the pervasive social elements of the culture in which Jesus' parables were created is the "cultural code" of honor and shame. In the first century, a person of honor attains and maintains honor by conforming to traditional patterns of behavior.[9] As Malina and Neyrey succinctly summarize, "Honor is the positive value of a person in his or her own eyes plus the positive appreciation of that person in the eyes of his or her social group" (25–26). Honor includes one's publicly acknowledged social standing, which can be divided into three major areas: the appropriate ability to control others (power); appropriate male/female roles (sexual status); and appropriate relationship in the fixed hierarchy of superiors and subordinates.[10]

All interactions between people outside of the family setting are inherently connected to competition with others for recognition of one's "honor rating." Therefore honor may be acquired through a social dialectic of challenge and riposte.[11] As Malina and Neyrey note, even a public question initiates an honor/shame challenge, as the verses just preceding the parable of the Good Samaritan illustrate (Lk 10:25–29). The lawyer's question about eternal life is no innocent request for information; instead it is a challenge that puts Jesus "to the test" (10:25). As common in an honor/shame defense, Jesus responds with a question that puts the lawyer on the spot instead (10:26). The lawyer is forced to answer in a traditional fashion, so Jesus successfully withstands this honor challenge (51).

The lawyer is shamed by his unsuccessful challenge, so he asks a second question. Once again, he is trying to stump Jesus and recoup his own lost honor.[12] Note that he desires to "justify himself" when he asks, "Who is my neighbor?" (10:29). Jesus responds with the parable of the Good Samaritan and with another counter question concerning who, among the priest, Levite, and Samaritan, proved to be a neighbor (10:36). Once again, Jesus wins the honor/shame contest when the lawyer is forced to admit (albeit indirectly) that the Samaritan is the one who proved to be the neighbor by his merciful actions. Finally, the parable itself directly challenges the code of honor held by the members of Jesus' audience because it shockingly elevates a Samaritan outsider over Jewish priests and Levites as examples of covenant compassion (51).

William Herzog claims that a recognition of the social code of honor significantly alters our understanding of the Laborers in the Vineyard parable (Mt 20:1–16).[13] Previous interpreters negatively evaluated the voices of the complaining workers so that the action of the owner of the vineyard symbolized God's gracious, generous goodness (82). Herzog proposes instead to divest the parable of theological accretions to focus more clearly on the social world depicted: the agrarian world of rural Galilee and Judea.

The characters of the parable are not abstract theological types but belong to identifiable social groups in advanced agrarian societies. The landowner is a member of the urban elite who owns a large estate that produces a great harvest. The day laborers, on the other hand, are members of the "expendable" class who live at or below subsistence level.[14] Although the wealthy landowner has a steward as retainer, Jesus portrays him as hiring the workers directly to depict a direct confrontation between these two social groups. They represent the two extremes of agrarian society: a ruthless and exploitative landowner and the poor, desperate peasants who are fighting a losing battle of survival (90).

Herzog argues that when the last-hired workers are paid first, the landowner deliberately insults the first-hired workers. Because he pays the workers who worked just one hour the same as the workers who toiled all day, he shames the labor of the first-hired (20:8–10), and they respond to his provocation (20:11–12). Therefore, the wage settlement initiates an honor/shame contest with the steward delivering the insult (20:8). The workers, however, fight to maintain their meager position in society. The episode concludes with the final riposte from the shrewd but exploitative landowner (20:13–15) who feigns courtesy with a

condescending form of the word "friend," banishes the spokes-
person of the workers with an "evil eye" accusation, and blas-
phemes by asserting his control over what should properly be
seen as Yahweh's land (94). The landowner thus demonstrates his
sinful allegiance to the aristocratic view of the elites: Despising
peasants enabled them to rationalize their exercise of power over
these "expendables" and to justify their exploitation (69). So this
parable, instead of using the landowner as a symbol for God, cod-
ifies the incongruity between the coming reign of God and the
earthly systems of oppression that pretend to be legitimate
guardians of its values (97).

John H. Elliott's analysis of the "Evil Eye" in this parable
provides a different interpretation.[15] Belief in the Evil Eye
includes the notion that certain individuals had the power to
injure another person just by a glance. Because the foremost
malevolent emotion associated with the Evil Eye was envy,
Elliott believes that the parable contrasts divine compassion with
invidious human comparison: An Evil Eye accusation (20:15) is
employed to denounce envy as incompatible with life in the kingdom of heaven (52–53).

Elliott believes that the landowner appropriately contrasts
his goodness with the evil of his accusers and deservedly shames
them by exposing their "Evil-Eyed envy" (60–61). Such envy
manifests a failure to comprehend God's benefactions, an unwill-
ingness to renounce "business as usual," and a refusal to rejoice in
the blessings of others. Thus, for Elliott, the householder represents God: The story illustrates the unlimited favor of God, con-
demns Evil Eye envy as incompatible with social life as governed
by the rule of God, and affirms Jesus' solidarity with the poor and
undeserving (61–62).

The analyses by Herzog and Elliott appear incompatible,
and Herzog's interpretation seems closer to demonstrating Jesus'
solidarity with the poor. In my view, however, the differences primarily stem from the ideological perspective taken on a social-
scientific level: Elliott's analysis is closer to an "emic"

perspective—an interpretation that centers more on the viewpoint, categories of thought, and explanations of the group being studied.[16] Herzog's interpretation, on the other hand, even though it evaluates the first-century social contexts, comes from a more "etic" perspective—the perspective and classifying systems of an external investigator.

Elliott focuses on the pervasive notion of the Evil Eye and its implications for the story, especially in its Matthean context. Herzog, on the other hand, openly declares his etic agenda, in part by speaking of the "peril of not modernizing Jesus."[17] He believes that it is important to minimize our anachronizing tendencies, but it is also crucial to acknowledge that every interpretation "modernizes Jesus." Such modernizing is not only unavoidable, but it is absolutely necessary to make Jesus' teachings understandable and relevant to modern persons.

Thus Herzog utilizes Paulo Freire's "pedagogy of the oppressed" to assert that the "social construction of reality" of peasants was dependent on the elites in their society. In other words, peasants internalize the world as understood by their oppressors because the elite deposit their worldview in the peasants' minds and hearts (e.g., through dominant language patterns). It takes a new vocabulary and "outside teachers" to bring peasants to realize their situation and to facilitate building a new social construction of reality (19–21). For Herzog, Jesus served as this type of "outside facilitator" because his parables were designed to stimulate social analysis and to expose the contradictions between the actual situation of their hearers and the Torah of God's justice (28).

Ancient Economies: Limited Good and Patron-Broker-Client Relationships

Because most persons in the first-century Mediterranean world lived on a subsistence level, this lack of sufficient goods helped to generate and sustain the idea that all resources were limited, in short supply, and already distributed. In addition, most people were at the mercy of power-holders outside their social realm. Their sense of powerlessness was reinforced by the rugged climate and lack of natural resources available to them in many areas of the Mediterranean world, which also led to the belief that *all* positive values (e.g., honor, love, power) were also "limited goods."

This belief in limited good resulted in a system of horizontal and vertical reciprocal relationships to ensure social stability—an honorable person did not want to be seen as improperly attaining any social or material advantage. Vertical alliances were built around patron-client relationships. A patron has social, economic, political, or religious resources that are needed by a client; in return a client expresses loyalty or honor to the patron. A mediator between these two parties functions as a "broker."

As Halvor Moxnes demonstrates, patron-client relations are reflected in several of Jesus' parables.[18] The Lukan parable of the nobleman who went abroad and the servants/clients who served him well (19:11–27) is typical of patron-client relations between central power and peripheral vassals. The parable of the dishonest steward (16:1–9) tells the story of a landowner's client who served as a broker between the landowner and the tenants. The steward uses his position as broker to establish patron-client links between himself and his master's tenants. When he reduces their debts, they become indebted to him and thus obliged to receive him as a guest in his (future) time of need. Moxnes concludes that such parables clearly show the dependent relationship of the villagers to a central ruler and/or to rich absentee landlords in the cities. Because the distance (social and otherwise) between village and the center is so vast, there is little direct contact; an intermediary is needed, and this broker becomes an important figure. This role is so important that it is also used as a model for the leadership within the Jesus community.

This model of leadership in the Christian community is possible because God is the ultimate patron and Jesus is depicted as the broker of God's blessings to the people. But in the parable of the Wedding Feast (Lk 12:35–40) a paradox appears: the master (patron) takes the role of a servant (12:37). Jesus here and elsewhere identifies greatness with serving, rather than being served. The result is a transformation of the traditional concept of patronage (258–59), and it bypasses the established urban and legal central power of Temple and Torah by proclaiming the immediacy of the kingdom of God (265).

Ancient Economies: Peasant Readings/ Hearings of the Parables

Douglas Oakman cogently argues that Jesus' words and actions articulate a coherent response to first-century economic realities.[19] Jesus critiqued both the peasant ethos of self-sufficiency and the exploitative redistribution of the Temple in Jerusalem.

In antiquity, economic exchanges within and between villages were based on reciprocity (exchange by gift or barter). The larger "political economy," however, was characterized by redistribution—the politically or religiously induced extraction of a percentage of local production from the powerless to the powerful (e.g., taxes, tithes, or rents). The Temple in Jerusalem, as one agent of redistribution, existed as a powerful means of exploitation that threatened ancient economic values through the impoverishment of the peasant population and that heightened tensions between elites and nonelites. Because peasants were left struggling to maintain their lives at a bare subsistence level, they were often forced to curtail consumption or enter into a hopeless, downward spiral of debt. Such oppression disturbed the reciprocal economic relations within villages and promoted what Oakman calls a "survivalist mentality" (78–80) because of the narrow margin between subsistence and starvation.

A peasant's view of "the good life" revolved around three interrelated values: a reverent attitude toward the land, strenuous agricultural work as good (but commerce as bad), and productive industry as a virtue.[20] Jesus created his parables within the context of these peasant realities (100–102). Yet Jesus—because he was a peasant artisan (a carpenter)—also had social contacts and familiarity with the social circumstances of the wealthy. Many of the parables thus demonstrate a detailed knowledge of large estates, the behavior of slaves and overseers, and other economic aspects of the elite.[21]

The parable of the Sower, for example, agrees with the peasant view of the primary producer in an immediate relationship with God. The sower is not negligent, as some modern interpreters suggest; instead God provides the harvest in spite of all the natural, inimical forces that threaten the crop. But through this parable Jesus critiques the peasant values of frugality and strenuous labor by declaring that God will provide the harvest (107–9). The providence of God is also clearly seen in the parable of the Darnel Among the Wheat (Mt 13:24–30), which invites nonelites to stop "hoeing" and to wait for the imminent reign of God (129). This advice, once again, undermines the values of Jesus' peasant audience, which focuses on frugality and hard work.

In the face of the exploitative urban elite (e.g., redistributive institutions such as the Roman state and Jewish Temple), the concentration of land holdings in the hands of a few, rising debt, and other destabilizing forces, Jesus responded by calling for a reversal of the centralization of political power and economic goods. In addition, Jesus advocated exchanges built on "general reciprocity"—giving without expecting anything in return (e.g., the remission of debts; 168). Such general reciprocity fosters unity and propitiates potential enemies, but, for Jesus, it also fosters the reestablishment of kinship among all peoples. Love for enemies is a corollary of this general reciprocity, which profoundly expresses human dependence on God's graciousness and willingness to provide for material human needs.

Oakman explores in a later work how the parable of the Good Samaritan epitomizes this love for one's enemies.[22] Because peasants were compelled to give up a precious amount of their hard-earned sustenance to outsiders, the common orientation of peasants was to distrust strangers—especially those who dealt in commerce. Outsiders were seen as possible threats to their existence or livelihood, and a cultural chasm existed between city dwellers (where landowners tended to live) and peasant villagers (118).

The parable of the Good Samaritan presupposes typical peasant valuations of the characters but does not simply identify with their interests. Peasant sympathies, Oakman argues, would have been with the bandits of this parable. Yet Jesus abhors the violence of the bandits while accepting some of the basic goals of banditry—justice and the securing of subsistence for the poor. In addition, most modern interpreters ignore the indications in the parable that the Samaritan was a trader—a profession despised by peasants. For Jewish peasants, the Samaritan is a cultural enemy (Samaritan), an evil man (a trader), and a fool. The Samaritan was foolish because he treated the injured man graciously as if he were a family member and was naive about the situation at the inn: Because inns were notoriously synonymous with crime and evil deeds, for this gullible Samaritan to trust the injured man to the care of such an evil place—and to give the innkeeper a blank check!—was a folly that could prove deadly to the injured person (122–23).

Oakman concludes that Jesus fully expected peasants to laugh all the way through this story. But Jesus compares the enormity of God's generosity to the actions of a hated foreigner of despised social occupation, and, in fact, God's mercy even reaches the point of danger and folly. God's kingdom is found in the most unlikely, even immoral, places. And God, like the Samaritan, is indebted to pay whatever may be required (123). As Oakman reiterates in another work,[23] the parable subverts traditional village morality and opens up the countryside to new possibilities: general reciprocity as characteristic of the kingdom of God and as a radical protest against the exploitative agrarian situation in early Roman Palestine (175).

The parable of the Good Samaritan creates a reversal of expectations. In a similar way, once we read these parables with (acquired) peasant eyes and hear them with peasant ears, our Western, postenlightenment interpretations of them are often reversed. Richard Rohrbaugh's "peasant reading" of the Parable of the Talents/Pounds illustrates this very well.[24] Modern interpreters often understand this parable as praise for "homespun capitalism" (33). Yet a modern market economy is completely foreign to ancient agrarian societies. The purpose of labor was not the creation of value but the maintenance of the family and the well-being of the village. Rohrbaugh explains how peasants, with a perspective of "limited good," would see the rich master in the parable as greedy to the core. In fact, from the peasants' viewpoint, the parable is a "text of terror" that confirms their worst fears about the kingdom of God: that it mirrors their daily lives in which the strong are rewarded for trampling on the weak (35). In addition, the third servant who protects the existing goods of the master (who is denigrated in modern interpretations) acts in the way that is most honorable in the eyes of peasants.

Thus, once again, social location helps to determine one's reading of the parable. The elite view the master as rightfully angry with the third servant, and Jesus is therefore warning about a lack of industry. To peasants, however, the master is terribly wrong in his rebuke, and Jesus is therefore admonishing the rich concerning their unholy reactions to peasant behavior (38).[25]

The Household, Gender Roles, and Parables' Portrayal of Women

Only nine female characters appear in a cast of 108 characters in the parables. This domination of male characterization in the parables cannot be easily brushed aside.[26] On the other hand, John H. Elliott demonstrates that the narrative of Luke-Acts contrasts the household with the Temple in Jerusalem.[27] The parable of the Pharisee and the Toll Collector depicts the Temple as the place where social and religious differences are demarcated; the household is the place where God's promises are realized (213–14). This contrast is seen throughout Luke-Acts: The Temple, with its exclusivist holiness ideology, hierarchical stratified social order, and exploitative economic redistribution proves incapable of mediating the inclusive salvation envisioned by the prophets. The households of Jesus' followers, though, are communities of "brothers and sisters" that embody repentance, faith, forgiveness, generosity, mercy, and justice, all within a social unity of generalized reciprocity (234–39).

In antiquity the household was the basic building block of society and the dominant economic unit. The household had important political, social, religious, and economic implications and became the model for social forms of communal life. A system of roles constitutes most family relationships inside the household, and Stuart Love's macrosociological analysis of the household in the Gospel of Matthew examines the role of gender in these relationships.[28] Matthew presupposes a rigid, hierarchical, authority-centered social structure largely based on the paradigm of the household. The social stratification in Matthew reflects the advanced agrarian society in which it was written, a society that has a crystallized, hierarchical, male-dominated social order (22). Within the marriage relationship, women are usually subordinate, seen as inferior to men, and possess few rights. The domestic care of the household is the wife's world in which she pleases her husband by preparing food and clothing, which enhances his status among his peers. The public realm, on the other hand, primarily belongs to men. Because of the separation of the public and private realms, women do not usually participate in political, educational, or public religious functions (23). Although Matthew presents some significant deviations from this gender-role norm, it does not burst the societal boundaries of the household (26–27).

In a later article, Love notes that although there were expected "public roles" for men and "private roles" for women in ancient societies, recent studies now stress the "complementarity" in these relationships. Women exercised "informal public power" (e.g., the use of gossip) to affect (indirectly) male public decisions and behavior (54).[29]

The kingdom of heaven parables in Matthew 13 are located "outside the house" (13:1) and then "in the house" (13:36), a public/private spatial distinction that divides the discourse. In both places, however, only the disciples enter into dialogue with Jesus; the crowds remain silent. The public teachings contain four parables that might have been for a "mixed multitude" (i.e., including women). The first three involve outdoor agricultural activities: the Sower (13:3–9, 18–23), the Weeds (13:24–30), and the Mustard Seed (13:31–32). The fourth, the Leaven (13:33), compares the growth of the kingdom to a domestic procedure, a woman hiding leaven in flour—a stereotypical feminine role. The teachings of Jesus to the disciples in private are appropriate for a male audience (60–61).

Even though the male disciples reflect the social realities of advanced agrarian societies and have the authority to teach and lead the church, there is an important difference: The paradigm for faith and service is found among women and other marginalized persons scattered throughout Matthew. This new male hierarchy, Love concludes, eschews patriarchal authoritarianism. The presence of women in the crowds opens a real but limited alternative: The Matthean Jesus acknowledges their presence, considers them worthy, treats them as persons, and receives their hospitality and ministry. Thus there exists a new inclusion in a hierarchy that is based on the old androcentric social framework, but, in Matthew, women unfortunately still "watch from a distance" (63).

Alicia Batten agrees that women in antiquity generally were the most active within the domestic realm, but she points to evidence that some women took on more public roles during the New Testament era.[30] In addition, she concurs that a woman in antiquity had some informal power over her husband and exercised limited control over his public actions (45). The woman orders the house, raises the children, and assumes many financial tasks. Most importantly, the woman upholds male honor not only through her sexual purity but also in acts of hospitality. In addition, she can subtly manipulate opinion by informal gossip networks in the village community—a type of power never acknowledged in male-authored literature (45).

In her study of the "Q source," Batten readily admits that its language is androcentric. Women appear hiding yeast in dough, grinding meal, and being married, but only as men see them. Yet parables concerning men are paired with parables concerning women (e.g., Mustard Seed; Leaven), which seems to be a deliberate attempt to address both men and women (47–48). Further, the parables of the Leaven and the Mustard Seed "liberate" these symbols from their "unclean" status by turning them into metaphorical ingredients of the kingdom of God. Indirectly, they place value on both the woman's and man's activity, which is especially significant because an acknowledgment of women's labor is unusual in patriarchal societies (48). Thus we catch parabolic glimpses of a more inclusive environment for women in a predominantly patriarchal society.[31]

Carol Schersten LaHurd also takes a cautiously optimistic view of these androcentric texts in her article concerning the "lost women" in the parables of Luke 15.[32] LaHurd rereads the parables of Luke 15 through the eyes of Arab Christian women in modern Yemen—a test case to demonstrate the rewards and difficulties inherent in applying contemporary models from cultural anthropology to New Testament texts. She encounters some striking differences in interpretations. In the parable of the Prodigal Son, for example, the Yemeni women had much more empathy with the older brother and observed that it was typical for the youngest child to be lazy and irresponsible. Even more striking was their interpretation of the father's actions. Most modern commentators stress the unexpected acceptance of the errant son when he returns. These women, however, understood the family as the location of unconditional care and were not surprised at the father running out to give his son a loving welcome (67). LaHurd surmises that these women see fathers "as they are, not so much as they wish to be seen" (70). The absence of female characters in the parable was also of little concern to these women. They viewed the mother's role as being inside the home, whereas it was the father's role to be "outside" and welcome the son back home.

LaHurd concludes that the negative assessments of the role and status of women in Luke's Gospel are significantly guided by Western cultural assumptions about what constitutes status and power for both men and women, as well as the modern tendency to give primacy to the public sphere (71). Peasant societies, in contrast, see household gender roles as complementary. Orderly household management and effective raising of children appear to have a worth equal to the more typically male role of earning the family income in the public realm. In such cultures women control some aspects of things most valued by men—honor, children, and a happy, well-organized household (72).[33]

Diane Jacobs-Malina, in her book *Beyond Patriarchy,*[34] argues that the image of Jesus presented in the gospels is analogous to the idealized role of the wife/mother (of the absent husband/father) because Jesus' primary role was to create and maintain the household of God on earth (1–2). The feminine/domestic aspects of the image of Jesus in the gospels have been suppressed by the selective inattentiveness of male scholars. A closer look demonstrates that Jesus found the idealized role of women to be more amenable to the designs of God: nurture, healing, and restoration. Thus he chose these values and goals that support the domestic sphere as the ones around which the (male) public sphere should be organized in relation to both men and women (117–118).

Jacobs-Malina's study provides an essential critique of the traditional, androcentric theological interpretations of Jesus' life and message. Similar assessments can be seen in the work of some of the male scholars mentioned above. Halvor Moxnes's investigation of the patron-broker-client relationship notes that Jesus transformed the traditional concept of patronage by identifying greatness with serving, rather than being served. Douglas Oakman describes the kingdom of God as being built on general reciprocity as a means of reestablishing kinship among all peoples. And John Elliott finds general reciprocity in the domestic associations of Acts within a community of "brothers and sisters."

All of these descriptions are imperfect analogies, but each one attempts to portray the image of a loving God who joyfully runs out to meet prodigal children. To most modern readers from the United States, the patriarchal household reflected in these texts is clearly oppressive to women. On the other hand, from a more emic perspective, women from modern Yemen can see their personal and social realities positively portrayed. As LaHurd observes, women and men socialized and educated in the industrialized West may not be the best judges as to what constitutes oppression in other societies (72). Yet, as Herzog notes, victims of oppression often internalize the world as understood by their oppressors even through the language system that is imposed upon them (19).

These complex issues cannot be decided here, but they are critical ones for modern interpreters of the parables. Some scholars, for example, still seek to reaffirm the patriarchal traditions found in biblical texts,[35] so these texts continue to be (ab)used to justify the oppression of women.

For a growing number of Christians, however, this approach is extremely inadequate, and the gap between these ancient texts and modern society grows wider. No longer can many Christians depend on cultural analogies of ancient societies to portray the activity of God. Yet the standards of the kingdom of God as depicted in Jesus' parables, although incorporating elements of that patriarchal system, actually provide a devastating critique of that system. Those higher standards, even while seen within their social system, may also serve as criteria by which all social systems are to be evaluated.[36] In the words of Elizabeth Schüssler-Fiorenza: "Thus liberation from patriarchal structures is not only explicitly articulated by Jesus but is in fact the heart of the proclamation of the *basileia* of God."[37]

Conclusion

We utilize models that give us partial glimpses of these ancient cultures—important glimpses that sometimes include the "voices of the silenced"—and these insights demonstrate the great cultural differences that divide us from ancient Mediterranean peoples. Such knowledge is instructive but can be destructive in the sense that previous suppositions and "certainties" are torn down. But what then? The gap between then and now has widened, and as Carolyn Osiek states, "the bridge is not long enough" to cross the interpretive chasm (113).

On the other hand, as Osiek also notes, for non-Western persons the cultural and social contexts may suddenly become more familiar now that the Western, postenlightenment framework undergirding most New Testament study is illuminated and (partly) dismantled. We do not have to anachronize Jesus' parables to make them relevant. The challenge is to modernize them authentically.

Social-scientific criticism allows us to understand better the first-century social, cultural, and historical contexts of the parables, but part of what it also teaches us, as do recent literary approaches, is that achieving the status of an "objective observer" is an elusive chimera that can never be captured by any interpreter. Pieces of the puzzle will still be missing; parables remain recalcitrant and delightfully enigmatic. But armed with the knowledge gained from social-scientific criticism, we can begin to understand the writings from other cultures and ages more fully and can avoid much of the patronizing interpretations that have pervaded many studies in the past.

7
From Simile and Metaphor to Symbol and Emblematic Language

The debates concerning allegory, simile, metaphor, and parable have been center stage in research on the parables, but in recent years the terms of the debates have shifted. Adolph Jülicher's insistence that similes/parables are expanded comparisons but that allegories are expanded metaphors was reversed; scholars such as Amos Wilder and Robert Funk maintain that similes/parables are extended metaphors and are not extended comparisons. In brief, the "meaning" of a parable is inherent in its metaphorical structure and unfolding images, a metaphorical process that transforms a reader.[1]

These latter studies on parable and metaphor most certainly overromanticized metaphor, but, as noted in chapters 2 and 3, a decisive shift in scholarly discussions had occurred. This shift can also be clearly illustrated by the debates surrounding parables and the kingdom of God, and, in these debates, the work of Norman Perrin plays a pivotal role. His pilgrimage is paradigmatic because his writings clearly demonstrate the move from discussions about the nature of the kingdom (e.g., his 1963 book *The Kingdom of God in the Teaching of Jesus*) to explorations of the nature of parable and of language about the kingdom (e.g., his 1976 book *Jesus and the Language of the Kingdom*).[2] In the latter volume, Perrin envisions the kingdom of God as the ultimate referent of all the parables of Jesus, but he also decisively states that the kingdom of God is a *symbol* because it can represent or evoke a whole range or series of conceptions (see below). Current discussions may disagree with Perrin's conclusions, but most studies involve explorations including other kinds of language. The debate now is the *kind* of thing that parable does—explorations that examine (or assume) aspects concerning the nature of language, including emblematic language. Therefore, discussions about the relation of parable and kingdom must also include an examination of the implications of the language one uses—which involves the relation of metaphor, allegory, parable, and the kingdom of God.

Parables and the Evolutionary Kingdom of God

Adolph Jülicher insisted that Jesus' central message was the kingdom of God. His conception of the kingdom of God in Jesus' parables, however, was dependent on nineteenth-century liberalism's assessment of the kingdom of God: a progressive, human development toward a more just social order on earth under the "fatherhood" of God.

Biblical studies in this era were dominated by the "social liberalism" of Albert Ritschl and Adolf von Harnack.[3] Ritschl believed in an evolutionary kingdom of God, one in which Jesus gave human beings responsibility to create a new society here on earth that would be fulfilled by an eternal kingdom after death. Human beings, in response to the rule of the kingdom in their hearts, were to work to establish God's kingdom on earth.[4] Ritschl, therefore, interpreted the "parables of growth" in this evolutionary way: The "Seed Growing Secretly" (Mk 4:26–29) portrayed the seed of Jesus' teaching as it was sown in the first century. It would grow and come to fulfillment in history as a result of human beings' response and faithfulness to the redemptive activity of God in Christ and of the human activity made possible by God's action.[5]

Most New Testament scholars still generally agree that the kingdom (reign) of God was a central message of the historical Jesus and his parables.[6] Yet significant differences remain concerning the "kingdom of God" and how the parables of Jesus illustrate, portray, or lead one to experience that kingdom.

Parables and the Imminent Apocalyptic Kingdom of God

In 1892 Johannes Weiss launched a broadside against the conception of the evolutionary kingdom of God with his *Die Predigt Jesu vom Reich Gottes.*[7] His study of Jewish apocalyptic literature convinced him that Jesus' message of the kingdom of God was apocalyptic. Far from being the gentle teacher proclaiming the fellowship of brothers and sisters under the protection of God the father, Jesus was an eschatological prophet who proclaimed the imminent end of the world. The coming of the kingdom was seen as wholly future, and human beings could do nothing to bring about the reign of God except to prepare for its imminent arrival. In addition, Weiss believed that many parables had nothing to do with the kingdom of God, and he rejected the parables as a reliable source for Jesus' understanding of the kingdom (60–64). Ironically, Weiss's book had almost apocalyptic repercussions in the scholarly community, and it set the stage for future discussions about the function and meaning of Jesus' parables.

Parables and the Presently Realized Kingdom of God

The apocalyptic understanding of the kingdom of God initially created a storm of protest, but in 1927, thirty-five years after the publication of Weiss's first book, the apocalyptic context became largely an accepted tenet.[8] At this point, C. H. Dodd entered this debate. Dodd utilizes Gustav Dalman's work on the rabbinical concept of the kingdom of God to argue that God's sovereignty could be realized in human experience by submission to the divine will.[9] Dodd believes that all the "eschatological parables" originally were told during a time of stress inherent in the ministry of Jesus. They were intended as an appeal for people to recognize that the kingdom of God was "present in all its momentous consequences." It was their conduct in the presence of this "tremendous crisis" by which they would judge themselves as either faithful or unfaithful, wise or foolish (130). Thus, although Jesus employed the "traditional symbolism of apocalypse" to indicate the absolute character of the kingdom of God, he used parables to express the idea that the kingdom of God "had come upon [them] there and then" (147).[10]

Brad Young also speaks of God's reign as a present reality among those who have accepted the call to obey the divine will, but he rejects the kingdom of heaven (God) as an eschatological concept designed to forewarn of an imminent catastrophe.[11] Young stresses that Jesus felt the dynamic force of God's reign as a present reality in his ministry. Like the rabbis, Jesus connected the "yoke of the kingdom" to repentance and obedience to God's commands. In the parables, however, the connection of this present reality to the secondary theme of the kingdom of a "future monarchy" to be established by God "does not appear to have originated with Jesus" (221). Jesus' message of the kingdom of heaven focused primarily on the power of his ministry of liberation, obedience to the divine will, and the people who became his disciples. The demands of the kingdom are simple yet difficult: complete surrender to the will of heaven. Like the parables of the Mustard Seed and the Leaven, this dynamic power will continue to grow when people respond to this call for total obedience (221).

Young's discussion of the kingdom of heaven and the parables is limited to a carefully-selected number of parables that accentuate the present reality of the kingdom and, like Dodd, Dalman, and others, his use of rabbinic literature is anachronistically suspect. Rabbinic traditions are often very difficult to date, and we cannot assume that they accurately portray beliefs contemporary with Jesus.[12]

Parables and the Partially Realized Kingdom of God

Dodd's "Realized Eschatology" created yet another round of eschatological jousting concerning Jesus' conception of the kingdom of God, but soon a consensus developed. Most scholars opted for a variation of what Joachim Jeremias called "eschatology in the process of realization" and concluded that there were both "realized" and "unrealized" aspects of the kingdom in the teaching of Jesus. Scholars such as Norman Perrin argued that there was "a tension between the Kingdom as present and the Kingdom as future, between the power of God as known in the present and the power of God to be known in the future."[13] In this view, Jesus not only was the harbinger of the kingdom, but also in some sense embodied the presence of that kingdom. Major works incorporating variations of this view include those by Norman Perrin (from 1963 until 1974),[14] W. G. Kümmel,[15] Aloysius Ambrozic,[16] George Eldon Ladd,[17] and George Beasley-Murray.[18]

George Beasley-Murray, for example, explores how parables contribute to this understanding of Jesus and the kingdom of God. Parables of Jesus concerning the coming of the kingdom of God in the present include the parable of the Sower (e.g., Mk 4:1–9), which not only portrays the kingdom of God coming into the world in spite of unfavorable circumstances, but also depicts the mission of the kingdom of God—its operation in the world, being opposed in a variety of ways but coming in spite of all with fullness of blessing (128–31). The kingdom had come quietly and had made its beginning in the face of opposition, but its continuance is assured until the glorious harvest. The parable of the Tares (Mt 13:24–30) illustrates that Jesus' current task was not to mediate the judgment of God but to be the agent of the redemptive powers of the kingdom. Jesus' confidence in the sovereignty of God leads him to leave the future judgment up to God (132–35). The parables of the Mustard Seed and Leaven contrast the inconspicuous nature of the initiation of God's rule in the ministry of Jesus with the great end to which it leads. The parable of the Seed

Growing Secretly also includes the assurance that what has begun with Jesus will inexorably lead to the final culmination of the kingdom of God. But Jesus emphatically states in these parables that the kingdom is not in the future only: God's sovereign action is even now operative in Jesus' words and actions.[19]

Yet all of the above parables, Beasley-Murray argues, also reflect Jesus' belief in the coming of the kingdom of God in the future. Other parables primarily focus on this future aspect. The parable of the Burglar (Mt 24:43–44/Lk 12:39–40) sets forth the unexpectedness of the parousia, and it calls for "readiness" on the part of all (209–12). The parable of the Wise and Foolish Maidens (Mt 25:1–13) sends a similar message: The people of God must be prepared for the Lord's coming (212–15). The parable enjoins readiness for an event of which the time is not known but may be very near.[20] As the parable of the Talents illustrates, for example, the proclamation of the kingdom challenges God's people to become what they were meant to be: the salt of the earth and the light of the world. Although Beasley-Murray allows for the significant amount of redaction evident in the two versions of this parable in Matthew and Luke, he argues that the plot itself— specifically the *absence* of the master and his *return*—demands that the "rendering of accounts" is essential to this parable. So the separation of the master from the servants means that the picture of the parable is not possible at all apart from a certain parousia expectation (218).

Parables and the Atemporal Kingdom of God

Norman Perrin continuously challenged his colleagues with bold new positions on methodology and interpretation, and his openness to innovative approaches still provides both a challenge and an inspiration to New Testament scholars.[21] Until the spring of 1974, Perrin was a champion of "partially realized eschatology" and had written one of the definitive works on Jesus' conception of the kingdom of God.[22] But in his book *Jesus and the Language of the Kingdom,* Perrin changes course dramatically. His new perspective approaches the kingdom of God as a symbol with deep roots in Jewish self-identity as the people of God that functions within the context of the myth[23] of God active in history on behalf of God's people. By the time of Jesus, it had come particularly to represent the expectation of a final eschatological act of God (40). Perrin argues that most such apocalyptic symbols are "steno-symbols"—which have a one-to-one relationship to what they represent—whereas Jesus' use of the kingdom of God was a "tensive symbol"—which has a set of meanings that can neither be exhausted nor adequately expressed by any one referent.[24] This usage reflects its earlier application in ancient Judaism (31).

Perrin declares that the kingdom of God was the "ultimate referent of all the parables of Jesus." He agrees that parables are metaphors, in that "they were bearers of the reality with which they were concerned and that the parables of Jesus mediated to the hearer an experience of the kingdom of God" (55–56). That is why Perrin declares that the kingdom of God is a *symbol* because it can represent or evoke a whole range or series of conceptions (33). *Concept* reflects cognitive aspects that can be explicitly stated in discursive speech. *Symbol* is more experiential.[25]

The symbolic, metaphoric aspects of parables and the kingdom of God were echoed by Perrin's contemporaries (see chapters 2 and 3). Amos Wilder declares that a metaphor-parable imparts an image that directly conveys a vision of what is signified and that the kingdom parables mediated something of the faith of Jesus.[26] Robert Funk emphasizes that a parable as metaphor produces an impact on the imagination—it is "creative of meaning"—and induces a vision that "cannot be conveyed by prosaic or discursive speech." Parable is a bearer of the reality of the kingdom of God ("The kingdom of God **is,**" not "The kingdom of God **is like**") and has an "ecstatic mythical intensity" (per Wilder) that transcends and dissolves common temporal categories.[27] For Dan Otto Via, parables as aesthetic objects impart a new vision of human existence and as biblical texts communicate the nature of faith: Specifically, the eight true narrative parables are metaphors of the kingdom of God and give a vision of existence as transacted by the surprising incursion of the kingdom."[28] John Dominic Crossan asserts that parables present the kingdom of God as "permanent eschatology," the permanent presence of God as the one who challenges world and repeatedly shatters its complacency.[29]

Bernard Brandon Scott's first book explores the relationship between parables and the kingdom of God.[30] Scott argues that parables are generated from Jesus' experiential world and give his fundamental vision of reality. To enter the world of parable is to enter a new horizon that seeks to orient one to the kingdom of God. Through a metaphorical "insight"—which cannot be reduced to discursive speech or propositions—one understands that the "referent of the symbol kingdom of God is an ultimate who makes ultimate claims upon human experience" (175). Jesus' language creates for its receiver a perspective that "impels faith"—a faith in Yahweh and implicitly a faith in Jesus as the symbol maker for Yahweh, and the presiding symbol of this perspective is kingdom of God (177).

Scott's *Hear Then the Parable* returns to the subject of "Parable and Kingdom" (56–62). He claims that "kingdom of God," as symbol, is *nebula,* indistinct, unformed content that cannot be coded with specificity (58). But people try to "domesticate" this *content nebula* through such things as allegory, an "overcoding of a symbolic text to establish authority over the text so that its content will not be *nebula* but known" (58). In a similar way, interpreting Jesus' use of *kingdom of God* as an apocalyptic concept is also an "overcoding" of the symbol; it can be used that way, but it actually opens onto a much wider spectrum (i.e., it is, as symbol, "polyvalent"). Jesus' use of the term does conjure up the metaphor "God is a king" in its "structural network," but in the Jesus tradition, the relation is frequently "diaphoric": Jesus' discourse changes or challenges the implied structural network of associations (61). Scott closes by alluding to *Midrash Rabbah* on the Song of Songs: Parables are handles on the symbol of the kingdom of God. They enfold and encompass the symbol: "By means of parable one penetrates to the mystery of the kingdom— but only in parable" (62).

Allegory Reconsidered: Allegory, Metaphor, and Parable

Many scholars have cautioned against a romantization of metaphor and a denigration of allegory. Metaphor had been transformed from a literary figure into a theological and hermeneutical category that constituted both immediacy and transcendence. Scholars use language about parables encountering us as a Zen master encounters a pupil[31] and insist that, by definition, one can only speak of parables parabolically.[32] As John Donahue cautioned, "One hears phrases such as metaphor shattering worlds, creating new visions, and calling existence into question. The impression arises that at times salvation comes from metaphor alone!"[33]

Madeleine Boucher, for example, argues that the rhetorical dimension of parables should not be abandoned.[34] Boucher defines *parable* as "a story; this story conveys a lesson, so that the parable has a double meaning, the story and the lesson; the parable's purpose is to effect a change in the hearer, to lead to decision or action; and the lesson always is religious or moral" (17).

In Boucher's view, the assertion that parables are not allegories is both incorrect and misleading. Every parable has both literal and tropical (figurative) meaning. The direct, literal meaning is the story; the indirect, tropical meaning is its message or point. Because the message is only implicit or suggested indirectly, the hearer must deduce the lesson from the story (25–26). *Tropical* comes from the Greek word *trope,* which is a turn, change, or play on the meaning of words and always involves double meaning, but *allegory* is simply an extended metaphor in narratory form. Because allegory is not a literary genre or form, it is simply incorrect to speak of parable and allegory as two different and mutually exclusive literary genres or forms. Parable is a literary genre; allegory is not. Allegory is simply an element that may or may not be employed in the making of a parable. Every similitude or parable (except for example stories) is allegorical because each has both a literal and a metaphorical meaning (28–29).[35] Jesus' parables are primarily rhetorical (constructed to persuade), not primarily poetic (created to be contemplated or enjoyed). The two are not mutually exclusive, but any poetic elements are always subordinated to the parable's rhetorical function: Jesus' goal is to win over his audience to his view (32–37).

The emphasis on the function of metaphors/parables is, in part, a return to the classical view of a metaphor as a powerful and persuasive instrument of communication.[36] William Brosend, after a brief review of scholarship on *metaphor,* concludes that a "parable is not and cannot be a metaphor. At the closest one might echo Ricoeur's 'metaphorical process' or Scott's 'metaphorical network' as constituent of a parable, but to call a parable a metaphor is to confuse categories. A metaphor is a trope or rhetorical figure, a parable is a narrative form."[37]

And, as Mary Ford argues, the disdain and even hostility with which some interpreters hold allegory as "opposed to" metaphor is based on an outmoded view of allegory: "Allegory, now properly understood, has resumed a place of great respect in literary circles."[38] Numerous other studies echo these sentiments. Hans-Josef Klauck makes a clear distinction between *Allegorie* (a literary mode or rhetorical device that can be found in many literary genres), *Allegorese* (an interpretive method that produces hidden and often anachronistic extraneous meanings to a text), and *Allegorisierung* (the subsequent allegorical elaboration of a text in which allegorical elements are already present).[39] Jesus' parables certainly include allegory—extended metaphors that demand perception, engagement, and interpretation on the part of the audience. In fact, the subsequent allegorical elaboration of these parables is a necessary interpretive device that makes the texts relevant for later audiences. This process "allows the fading voice of the earthly Jesus to be brought to the hearing of the believing community as the *viva vox* of their Risen Lord" and "apart from *Allegorisierung* we would no longer possess Jesus' parables" (361).[40]

Parables and the Liberating Kingdom of God

Other scholars are exploring the *language* of the kingdom in ways that include more attention to Jesus' parables as social and ideological discourse. David Batstone suggests that people often overlook how ideologically explosive the "notion" of the kingdom of God was within Jesus' own culture.[41] He argues that, in first-century Palestine, it did not have the same metaphorical and "strictly religious" connotations that make the term so "safe" today. Modern interpreters have domesticated this evocation of the memory and impulse of the Yahweh who acts to deliver Yahweh's chosen ones from oppression. Thus Jesus' proclamation of the kingdom includes the conviction that history stands at the brink of a great reversal so that the unjust will no longer prosper and the chosen ones will no longer suffer (385).

William Herzog argues that to understand the connection between Jesus the teacher who spoke in parables and the "subversive" who threatened the ruling powers of the day, one must interpret the parables of Jesus as "subversive speech."[42] Parables tell us of the world in which the peasants and rural underclass lived, and Jesus' parables dealt with dangerous political and economic issues. These subversive parables exposed the contradictions between the actual situations of the hearers and the Torah of God's justice. Parabling was "risky business" because Jesus was unmasking and challenging the oppression of the poor by the ruling elite. Because Jesus' parables could incite peasants and villagers to social unrest or even revolt, the powerful would not take this challenge lightly; it would lead to Jesus' death (28).[43]

Allegory Reconsidered: The Semitic Context

Paul Fiebig, in his response to Jülicher, argued that Jesus' parables, like the rabbinic parables, had multiple points of comparison and were not free from allegory.[44] More recently, Raymond Brown, while expressing appreciation for Jülicher's contributions, noted that Jülicher's total rejection of allegory was an oversimplification because there "is really no sharp distinction between parable and allegory in the Semitic mind."[45] Jesus would have naturally used the simple allegories and metaphors already familiar to his listeners from the Jewish scriptures and elsewhere. In fact, some of the parables of Jesus "cry out for an allegorical interpretation" (38).

David Stern declares that the terms *parable* and *allegory,* as they have been used in scholarship, are simply not helpful in understanding the *mashal* (see chapter 4).[46] The *mashal* is a literary-rhetorical form that employs certain poetic and rhetorical techniques to persuade its audience of the truth of a specific message relating to an ad hoc situation. The features of a *mashal*—whether they be called allegorical or symbolic—exist only for the sake of enabling its audience to grasp for themselves the ulterior message that the *mashal* bears. The literary power of the parable as a "bearer of reality" has been overly romanticized by the parable-as-metaphor proponents. Stern eloquently decries this notion of parable as metaphor that "stands for a totalizing identification of literature *and* life, for speech as epiphany, for the parable as Logos" (12).

Allegory and Kingdom Reconsidered:
Parables as Poetic Fictions

Charles Hedrick wrote *Parables as Poetic Fictions*[47] when he discovered that his work was taking him out of the "mainstream" of parable interpretation (xi). Like Dan Otto Via's seminal work, Hedrick's study analyzes the parables as narrative fictions, but, unlike Via, he stresses the critical importance of the historical and cultural contexts of first-century Palestine (e.g., 79–80). Hedrick assumes that the parables of Jesus are ordinary stories, brief, freely invented, fictional narratives that realistically portray aspects of first-century Palestinian life (3–5). In part, this assumption is based on Via's argument that parables are aesthetic objects that refract a view of human existence and are not (primarily) metaphorical reflections of the kingdom of God. Instead, they are occasional partial "descriptions" of Jesus' poetic view of reality that offer auditors/readers a new way of viewing reality and new ways for them to make discoveries about themselves.[48]

Therefore Hedrick argues that readers of Jesus' parables should not begin by initially regarding them as images that are consciously designed to take readers outside the story to find relevant "meanings" in theological abstractions. Hedrick does not deny that Jesus' overall message may have been concerned in some degree with the kingdom of God, but because we do not know how he used these stories, we must start with the story itself rather than the kingdom of God (31). Readers are not authorized to go outside the world of the story or to use nonstory "referential" language to "interpret" the story *unless it is mandated by particular semantic markers in the story itself,* which, Hedrick contends, rarely occurs.[49] Hedrick believes that to assume that the stories were designed to take the reader to a specific point of reference outside the story is to treat the story as an allegory, which ultimately reduces the narrative to a discardable husk (35). In addition, the evangelists' literary settings lead readers astray and hamper their engagement of the stories as "first-century fictions" (3) and "ordinary stories" (4). As Hedrick aptly declares: "Hence, these tales of Jesus mean exactly what they say—and maybe more" (32).

Allegory *Redivivus:* Allegory and the Voice of Jesus

Joachim Jeremias had declared that the parables of Jesus had undergone a certain amount of reinterpretation by the early church and the gospel authors. His "principles of transformation" included the fact that allegorization increased due to the parables' later use as exhortation (see chapter 1 above). Scholars who basically follow Jeremias's approach are thus more likely to designate allegorical elements in the parables as the creation of either the early church or the gospel authors.

Craig Blomberg, however, seeks to demonstrate that the parables are both allegorical and authentic.[50] Armed with that conclusion, he critiques aspects of modern "mainstream" scholarship: form criticism (71–99), redaction criticism (101–31), and literary criticism (133–63). Blomberg's analysis, though sometimes helpful, underestimates the usefulness of the methodologies he critiques and minimizes their impact on the authenticity of sections of the gospels.[51]

Blomberg's interpretations of individual parables are structured around the tenuous assumption that "each parable makes one point per main character" (163)—which is later restated to assert that the triadic structure of most of Jesus' narrative parables suggests that they may make three (propositional) points, though some will make one or two (166). As Blomberg realizes, though, "the rhetorical power of the narratives is obviously lost by means of propositional paraphrase, as is a portion of their meaning" (293).[52]

John Sider builds on the foundation of Blomberg's work but approaches the parables in a different way.[53] Sider believes that "every parable is an analogy" (18)[54] and defines *parable* as "a discursive or narrative analogy in the service of moral or spiritual argument" (84). Almost all of Jesus' parables convey their meaning by elaborating one proportional analogy (illustrated by the mathematical formula $A:B = a:b$). Using the parable of the Lost Son as an example (Luke 15:11–32), this means that sinners relate to God in a way analogous to how the lost son relates to his father (sinners:God = lost son:father), with a series of related analogies (Pharisees:God = elder son:father; Pharisees:sinners = elder son:lost son).[55] The analogy compares the author's *tenor* or theme (sinners and God) with the author's chosen *vehicle* (the lost son and his father). The meaning of the comparison depends on some specific *point of resemblance* between the tenor and vehicle (e.g., the relationship between the lost son and his father in comparison with sinners and God). Sider further argues that one analogy is almost inevitably multiplied into several, and parable becomes allegory because every allegory is an elaboration of analogy (19). Therefore, almost all of Jesus' parables are allegories—where the comparison is elaborated beyond a single proportional analogy.

Sider's view that allegory is not a separate literary genre but a rhetorical device used in the service of argumentation allows us to focus on the rhetorical nature of parables. His "functional definition" of a parable (see above) allows parables to have a "pervasive intuitive force" yet does not envision them as a "very peculiar kind of poetic language" that tries to escape denotation. Sider argues that if we examine parables as argument, it can open up new possibilities for our intuitive response as well (84).

Conclusion: Parable, Metaphor, and Emblematic Language

In his book *The Matthean Parables,* Ivor Jones takes an extremely insightful, nuanced, and balanced approach, one which judiciously incorporates many of the points made in recent scholarship. Jones argues that metaphor can operate in different ways and that one single relationship between metaphor and "parable" is not to be assumed—some parables are not in the strict sense metaphorical at all; some, as narrative fiction, are closer to the pattern of a fable (68). The interrelationship between parable and context is intriguingly complex; for example, literary categories play a role—the novel, the play, the poem, the dialogue, and so forth. The social contexts of the one who speaks and the one who hears are both critically important (66). But, contrary to Sider and similar to Stern, Jones argues that there is a distinction between metaphor/parable and analogy. Metaphor relies on established *dissimilarities* between the things compared—the language "stretches" for these new applications and demands from the hearers an "imaginative strain"—whereas analogy downplays the differences and no "imaginative strain" is required (67).[57]

Allegorical language—or as Jones prefers, "emblematic" language—is "unavoidable" in parables simply because of their nature. It was just as natural for Jesus to use emblematic language as it was for ancient Jewish prophets to do so. Allegory in itself no longer provides a means of distinguishing authentic Jesus material from inauthentic; it was a feature of the parables from the beginning (79). Yet Jones also makes clear that the presence of allegory "from the beginning" does not mean that we can be confident that the parables reflect the level of Jesus' "authentic" message: "The complexity of the history of tradition makes the journey back long and uncertain, and all the more so now, because all of the signposts which Jeremias attempted to set up have had to be removed" (81). Jones believes that a detailed identification of an authentic tradition is "extremely hazardous," and the "living voice" of Jesus would only be identifiable (and only then with great difficulty) if the Jesus tradition from start to finish were hermetically sealed off from all other influences (before, during, and after). We are dealing with a range of narrative languages—those available to Jesus, to the early Christian communities, to the narrators of the stories, and to the hearers. These influences ring a "death knell" to any attempt to isolate an "authentic voice." The performance is not a solo, but a chorus of contributors (101–2).

Jesus' parables can create a fresh horizon for us because they expressed Jesus' perception of God and the world. His metaphors challenged the commonplace beliefs of his hearers by using language in a creative, nonconventional sense and invited them to revise their understanding of God's rule as well as their views of values, practice, and humanity. This new and challenging language opened the way for others of his own community whose linguistic conventions were different. They followed in his steps, found ways to keep his words alive in different contexts, and contributed to the shaping of cultural webs whose strengths can still be felt today. They responded in their own language and culture and in terms of their own community's life and practice (105). I would argue that although these beliefs may tell us little—or a lot—about the historical Jesus, they definitely speak volumes about the power and polyvalency of his parables.

Jones, in effect, recognizes many of the points I made at the end of chapter 3. The author of each gospel provides a rejoinder to Jesus' parables, but parables still call for dialogic responses on the parts of their hearers/readers. There are no spectators in the dialogic world of parable. The action is moved out of the horizon of the person performing the action in the past and is placed within the horizon of its contemplator.[58] Every event, every phenomenon, every thing that is represented parabolically, when it comes into contact with the present through a retelling of the story, becomes part of our world-in-the-making; it acquires a relationship—in one form or another and in one degree or another—to the ongoing event of our current life in which we are participating. In effect, it is an encounter of two authors.[59]

What this means is that even if we could ascertain the *exact* words (in Aramaic?) spoken by Jesus, the precise "original intention" still could not be recovered because even direct quotations can never be true repetitions of the original; the historical and cultural circumstances create a new situation and new connotations. The exact, original situation in Jesus' ministry is at the least unrepeatable and at the most unrecoverable.[60] The fact that the parables are embedded into a larger narrative makes this task even more impossible, because, as I noted at the end of chapter 3, this situation changes the parables' sense dramatically. In a complex relationship, the author's voice enters into a dialogue with the parable and reverberates throughout the rest of the narrative and narrative levels, and, in another complex relationship, the person who participates in understanding enters into the text or its hearing as a participant.

Conclusion

Recent parable scholarship has proved to be a creative and dynamic era in New Testament studies, possibly even the most exciting area of study in the discipline's long history. The vast array and diversity of approaches to the parables demonstrate that these brief narratives continue to challenge our hearts, minds, and imaginations. It sometimes appears that about the only item on which modern scholars seem to agree is that the historical Jesus sometimes spoke in parables.[1]

These dialogues in parable studies, though, are a sign of vitality and hope, and they certainly reflect the inherent nature of Jesus' parables. There are no spectators in the dialogic world of parable; all participate.Whether Hellenistic or Jewish in origin, parables have their roots in folklore, whose "little traditions" often parody elements of the ruling, dominant class.[2] Parables not only challenge and loosen the grip of established norms and relations in the dominant culture, but they contain and engender a criticism (and sometimes a mockery) of the official social order and ideology, and, as we have seen, parables can also vigorously critique "peasant culture" as well. Parables offer up instead another alternative: Jesus' view of reality.

But "parable," in its totality, does not reside alone in the creative genius of its author; it is a specific relation between creator and contemplators.[3] There is a complex correlation between text and contexts—the "original" context and the context which is being created as the text is read and reread. When we speak of parables, it is best not to speak of "meaning" because that closes off interpretation; it is much better to speak of "understanding." Understanding is a reinterpretation in a new context, so all true understandings of the parables are always historical, personal, and dialogical. As we "write" our own texts in response to the parables (see chapter 3 above), we strive for depth of insight, not accuracy of knowledge.

Communication in parable does not allow a passive role; the interlocutor participates in the formation of meaning as do, broadly speaking, the whole complex of social situations in which the utterance occurred. Parable can never be understood or explained outside of the link to the concrete situations of both the creator and hearer/reader. The hearer/reader is not like a telegraph operator who must decode and receive the original message and context. There is never a ready-made message that is transmitted from one to another; it is a construction, like an ideological bridge, that is constructed in the process of their interaction. In some sense, parables do not merely "reflect" situations; they assist readers in organizing situations and, indeed, transforming them. Also, parables in their polyvalency to an extent foresee and anticipate our responses; Jesus created them with one ear already attuned to our answers. Parables, therefore, are profoundly dialogic and do not pretend to be the last word because, in parable, the last word is continually granted to others....

Notes

Introduction

1. Note, for example, Origen's explanation of the parable of the Good Samaritan (Lk 10:30–37). He declares that the man traveling down the road represents Adam, and the Good Samaritan signifies Christ. The priest and the Levite symbolize the Law and the Prophets, respectively. Jerusalem is "paradise," and Jericho is "the world." The robbers symbolize the hostile influences of the world, and the man's wounds represent sins. The inn and its innkeeper represent the church and the angels in charge of the church, whereas the return of the Samaritan symbolizes the Second Coming of Christ (Origen, *Commentary on Luke* 10:30–35, Homily XXXIV). For a discussion of early allegorical interpretations of the parables, see Warren S. Kissinger, *The Parables of Jesus: A History of Interpretation and Bibliography* (London: The Scarecrow Press, 1979), 1–33; Robert H. Stein, *An Introduction to the Parables of Jesus* (Philadelphia: The Westminster Press, 1981), 42–47; and Lane C. McGaughy, "A Short History of Parable Interpretation (Part I)" *Forum* 8:3–4 (1995) 229–45.

2. Fyodor Dostoevsky, *Crime and Punishment*, trans. Richard Pevear and Larissa Volokhonsky (New York: Vintage Books, 1993).

Chapter One: Historical-Critical Approaches to the Parables

1. Jülicher revised this work, and a later two-volume edition came out in 1888 and 1889. The page references refer to the still

untranslated: *Die Gleichnisreden Jesu* (Darmstadt: Wissenschaftliche Buchgesellschaft, 1969).

In addition to my own reading of the scholarship mentioned in this analysis, I have utilized, in chapters 1, 2, and 3, the insights of the following discussions: Warren Kissinger, *The Parables of Jesus* (Metuchen, NJ: Scarecrow Press, 1979); Norman Perrin, *Jesus and the Language of the Kingdom* (Philadelphia: Fortress Press, 1976), 89–205; William A. Beardslee, "Recent Literary Criticism," in *The New Testament and its Modern Interpreters* (Philadelphia: Fortress Press, 1989); Timothy Noël, "Parables in Context: Developing a Narrative-Critical Approach to Parables in Luke," Ph.D. dissertation, Louisville, KY: The Southern Baptist Theological Seminary, 1986; James C. Little, "Parable Research in the Twentieth Century," *ExpT* 87:12 (1976) 356–60; 88:2 (1976) 40–43; 88:3 (1976) 71–75.

2. M. J. Lagrange ("La Parabole en dehors de l'Évangile," *Revue Biblique* 6 [1909] 198–212, 342–67) and Denis Buzy (*Introduction aux paraboles évangéliques* [Paris: Editions de l'Ecole, 1961]), for example, argue that this "essential" difference is not supported by Aristotle himself, nor by such rhetoricians as Quintillian.

3. C. H. Dodd, *The Parables of the Kingdom*, rev. ed. (Glasgow: Collins, 1961).

4. In Matthew it is one of the parables appended to the apocalyptic discourse taken from Mark (Mt 25:15–30). Luke, on the other hand, provides a brief but explicit introduction about the disciples thinking that the "kingdom of God was to appear immediately" (Lk 19:11; Dodd, 108–9).

5. Dodd insists that parables retain their imaginative and poetical quality: "They are works of art, and any serious work of art has significance beyond its original occasion....Their teaching may be fruitfully applied and re-applied to all sorts of new situations which were never contemplated at the time when they were spoken. But a just understanding of their original import in relation to a particular situation in the past will put us on right lines in applying them to our new situations" (146).

6. At a more complex literary level, Dodd's definition also conveys an important element that would later be used by literary critics such as Robert Funk: The parable as simile or metaphor "teases the mind into active thought" (see chapter 2 below).

7. I am using the eighth edition: *The Parables of Jesus* (New York: Charles Scribner's Sons, 1972). An abridged edition makes his work available to a wider circle of readers by omitting "the book's

purely technical and linguistic content": *Rediscovering the Parables* (New York: Charles Scribner's Sons, 1966), 9.

8. Here Jeremias stands on the shoulders of Jülicher and, more specifically, such scholars as B. T. D. Smith, who enumerates many of these conclusions in his *The Parables of the Synoptic Gospels* (Cambridge: Cambridge University Press, 1937), 40–59. Jeremias's list of transformations is as follows: (1) The parables were translated from Aramaic to Greek, which involved an inevitable change in meaning; (2) The "Palestinian" environment was translated into the "Hellenistic" environment; (3) Details were embellished; (4) The Hebrew Bible or folk-story themes influenced the shaping of stories; (5) The change of audience from opponents during the ministry of Jesus to the early Christian community; (6) A switch from an eschatological emphasis to exhortation; (7) The influence of the church's situation (e.g., the delay of the Parousia); (8) Allegorization increased due to the parables' later use as exhortation; (9) A tendency to collect and conflate (e.g., Mt 13); (10) Secondary contexts and frameworks as settings for the parables. In conclusion, Jeremias claimed that these ten laws of transformation are an aid to recovering "the actual living voice of Jesus" (114).

9. The titles of Jeremias's subsections clearly demonstrate these major emphases: (1) Now is the Day of Salvation; (2) God's Mercy for Sinners; (3) The Great Assurance; (4) The Imminence of Catastrophe; (5) It May Be Too Late; (6) The Challenge of the Hour; (7) Realized Discipleship; (8) The Via Dolorosa and Exaltation of the Son of Man; (9) The Consummation; (10) Parabolic Actions.

10. Even though the Jesus Seminar reaches significantly different results in its book *The Parables of Jesus*, it still follows three of Jeremias's basic assumptions: (a) the parables of Jesus were "distinctive instruments" of Jesus' speech; (b) the process of reinterpretation of Jesus' parables is obvious and related to their transmission in different situations and the encountering of new problems; (c) it is imperative to recover, as far as possible, the "genuine parables." See *The Parables of Jesus*, ed. Robert W. Funk, Bernard Brandon Scott, and James R. Butts (Sonoma, CA: Polebridge Press, 1988), 14–16. Cf. *The Five Gospels*, trans. and commentary by Robert W. Funk, Roy W. Hoover, and the Jesus Seminar (New York: Macmillan, 1993).

11. Norman Perrin notes concerning Jeremias's summary of the basic principles of Jesus' parables: "[T]his set of rubrics looks very

much like a summary of [Jeremias's] rather conservative Lutheran piety" (*Jesus and the Language of the Kingdom* [Philadelphia: Fortress Press, 1976], 106). Similar critiques, of course, can be leveled at every other study of the parables of the historical Jesus, including Perrin's.

12. John W. Sider, "Rediscovering the Parables: The Logic of the Jeremias Tradition," *JBL* 102 (1983) 61–83. Sider is much more sanguine about the reliability of the Synoptic contexts than I am, however. Plausible contexts are not necessarily authentic historical contexts.

13. Jack Dean Kingsbury, *The Parables of Jesus in Matthew 13* (London: SPCK, 1969).

14. I will use the titles given to the Synoptic Gospels, per convention, as designations of the "author," without any intention of specifying authorship to a particular historical person.

15. Charles E. Carlston, *The Parables of the Triple Tradition* (Philadelphia: Fortress Press, 1975).

16. *Kerygma* may be defined as the proclamation of the church "which tells of God's dealing in the man Jesus of Nazareth" (Perrin, *Jesus and the Language of the Kingdom,* 110). The literature is too vast to cite adequate treatments of this approach, but see Bultmann's *Theology of the New Testament*, 2 vols. (New York: Charles Scribner's Sons, 1951; 1955); *Jesus and the Word* (New York: Charles Scribner's Sons, 1934).

17. Bultmann saw this overconfidence as one of the primary mistakes of the scholars critiqued by Albert Schweitzer in *The Quest of the Historical Jesus* (New York: Macmillan, 1910).

18. As Perrin notes, Bultmann dismissed specific aspects of Fuchs's reconstruction as "an improbable psychological construction" (*Jesus and the Language of the Kingdom*, 109–10, 186).

19. Ernst Fuchs, *Studies of the Historical Jesus* (Naperville, IL: A. R. Allenson, 1964), 7.

20. Eta Linnemann, *Jesus of the Parables: Introduction and Exposition* (London: SPCK, 1966). The quote comes from Ernst Fuchs's introduction to the book (xi).

Chapter Two: The Emergence of Literary Approaches to the Parables

1. Wilder reminisces about these discussions in *The Bible and the Literary Critic* (Minneapolis: Augsburg Fortress, 1991), xi, 20–21.

2. Norman Perrin, *Jesus and the Language of the Kingdom* (Philadelphia: Fortress Press, 1976), 127.

3. Amos Wilder, *The Language of the Gospel: Early Christian Rhetoric*, rev. ed. (New York: Harper & Row, 1971). This larger context is also evident in his earlier works. See, for example, his (renamed) 1959 article, "The Symbolic Realism of Jesus' Language," which is found reprinted in *Jesus' Parables and the War of Myths*, ed. James Breech (Philadelphia: Fortress Press, 1982), 133–52.

4. Noted in Wilder's *The Bible and the Literary Critic*, xi.

5. Wilder makes an important distinction between a simile (which "compares") and a metaphor (which "reveals"). This lofty evaluation of the participatory aspects of metaphor inaugurated an era of parable study that tended to romanticize the power of "metaphor." See chapter 7 below.

6. A situation posited, in different contexts, by many previous scholars, such as Dodd, Jeremias, Fuchs, Linnemann et al. It is not surprising, then, that Wilder here quotes Fuchs approvingly (83).

7. A few later scholars, such as some members of the Jesus Seminar, would disagree—for a number of reasons—that these two elements can be reconciled. Instead, they posit a historical Jesus who is more like a Cynic sage than an eschatological prophet. For a brief discussion, see chapter 5 below. In addition, in chapter 4, I will point out that other scholars would argue that the terms *rhetorical perfection* and *formal uniqueness* may implicitly disparage the parables found in other religious traditions. This observation, however, does not impugn the religious and literary genius so easily seen in the parables of Jesus.

8. Once we reconstruct the "original forms" of the parables in Matthew 13 and Mark 4, for example, "we can feel with confidence that we hear Jesus of Nazareth speaking" (90).

9. Robert W. Funk, *Language, Hermeneutic, and the Word of God* (New York: Harper & Row, 1966).

10. A summary and analysis of parable research that focuses on the role of metaphor may be found in Mogens Stiller Kjärgaard,

Metaphor and Parable: A Systematic Analysis of the Specific Structure and Cognitive Function of the Synoptic Similes and Parables qua Metaphors (Leiden: E. J. Brill, 1986), esp., 133–97. See also the review by John Dominic Crossan in *JBL* 108 (1989) 148–50, and the article by James Champion, "The Parable as an Ancient and a Modern Form," *Journal of Literature & Theology* 3:1 (1989) 16–39. The theoretical underpinnings of this "Parable-as-Metaphor School" were provided by four main scholars: I. A. Richards, *The Philosophy of Rhetoric* (New York: Oxford, 1963); Philip Wheelwright, *Metaphor and Reality* (Bloomington, IN: Indiana University Press, 1962); Max Black, *Models and Metaphors* (Ithaca: Cornell University Press, 1962); and Paul Ricoeur, "Paul Ricoeur on Biblical Hermeneutics," *Semeia* 4 (1975) 29–148. See also Ricoeur's *The Rule of Metaphor*, trans. Robert Czerny (Toronto: University of Toronto Press, 1977).

11. Yet Funk maintains that "the Lukan context is...not inappropriate to the parable" (217) and that the disjunction between the lawyer's question (10:29) and the one asked by Jesus (10:36) was "necessary to the point" (221; cf. Jeremias, *The Parables of Jesus*, 205).

12. "The Good Samaritan as Metaphor," *Semeia* 2 (1974) 74–81.

13. Funk returns to this parable in *Honest to Jesus* (San Francisco: Harper, 1996), 170–80. Of note are the section on "Metaphorical Proclivities" and the reduction of the parable to the proposition: "In God's domain help is perpetually a surprise" (176–77, 180).

14. Via's literary analysis is therefore dependent upon the (then) current "New Criticism" of literary critics such as Murray Krieger, Northrop Frye, Elisco Vivas, William Wimsatt, Monroe Beardsley, and Philip Wheelwright.

15. Dan Otto Via, *The Parables: Their Literary and Existential Dimension* (Philadelphia: Fortress, 1967), 21–24.

16. Via is dependent upon Aristotle here (and Northrop Frye). In his analysis of eight Synoptic parables, Via discusses them in terms of three hyphenated rubrics: historico-literary criticism, literary-existential analysis, and existential-theological interpretation. The latter rubric was greatly criticized, so Via moves to a "literary-structural" approach in his *Semeia* 1 article (see below). Via does not define these rubrics, but see Norman Perrin's discussion in *Jesus and the Language of the Kingdom*, 148–49.

17. As Perrin notes, Via's important book gave parable interpretation a new dimension, but despite his methodological sophistication, his

conclusions have "a surprising amount of banality." Oddly enough, Via's conclusions sometimes amazingly echo Jülicher's. Instead of flowing naturally from the literary-existential analyses, Via's existential-theological interpretations regularly have a disconnected unclear relation to his aesthetic investigations. Perrin concludes, "There has to be more to the parables than that!" (*Jesus and the Language of the Kingdom*, 154). Perrin also notes that the dynamic interaction between text and interpreter deserves more attention (155).

18. Sallie McFague, *Speaking in Parables* (Philadelphia: Fortress Press, 1975).

19. Note McFague's statement about the "meaning" of the parable as an extended metaphor: "A parable is an extended metaphor. A parable is not an allegory, where the meaning is extrinsic to the story, nor is it an example story where, as in the story of the Good Samaritan, the total meaning is within the story. Rather, as an extended metaphor, the meaning is found only *within* the story itself although it is not exhausted by the story. At the same time a parable is an aesthetic whole and hence demands rapt attention on itself and its configurations" (13). She goes on to state that parable as metaphor shocks us into a new awareness, and that "if new meaning is always metaphorical, then *there is no way now or ever to have strange truth directly*" (41).

20. Mary Ann Tolbert, *Perspectives on the Parables* (Philadelphia: Fortress Press, 1979). In striking contrast to her predecessors, Tolbert argues that the presence of extraordinary elements "fractures" the realism of the narratives and leads one to conclude that parables as stories transcend a particular time or situation, which, in turn, encourages interpreters to seek other levels of meaning in them (89–91). Tolbert's views concerning "realism" are decidedly anachronistic, however. Cf. the critique by Charles Hedrick, *Parables as Poetic Fictions* (Peabody, MA: Hendrickson, 1994), 57–72.

21. Tolbert's "semiotic" model utilizes Susan Wittig's theory of multiple meanings; Tolbert's "rhetorical" model draws primarily from Philip Wheelwright's analysis of metaphor (35–49).

22. Tolbert provides two interpretations of the parable of the Prodigal Son, both of which stem from psychoanalytic (Freudian) theory. She concludes that one of those two interpretations is superior, however, because it better preserves the integrity of the story (111–14). Tolbert prefers the interpretation that is "guided by the surface struc-

ture" of the parable (114). Cf. Dan Via's Jungian analysis of the same parable: "The Prodigal Son: A Jungian Reading," *Semeia* 9 (1977) 21–43.

23. James Breech, *The Silence of Jesus: The Authentic Voice of the Historical Man* (Philadelphia: Fortress Press, 1983). The purpose of the parables is to communicate Jesus' "perception of, and attitude toward, human reality" (213).

24. As Charles Hedrick observes, this categorization is "refreshing" when compared to the subjective theological and thematic categories often used (e.g., by Jeremias), but Breech's categories fail to accommodate all the parables of Jesus for a number of reasons. See Hedrick's *Parables as Poetic Fictions*, 55–56.

25. The results of which were published in the first volume of *Semeia* in 1974.

26. Therefore it is derived from linguistic theory, not poetics. Robert Detweiler and Vernon K. Robbins state that structuralism "proclaims the linguisticality of existence." See their "From New Criticism to Poststructuralism: Twentieth-Century Hermeneutics," in *Reading the Text*, ed. Stephen Prickett (Cambridge: Blackwell, 1991), 253.

27. Structuralism can theorize about mythic structures (as in the work of Claude Lévi-Strauss) or narrative structure (as in the work of Vladimir Propp, Algirdas Greimas, and Claude Bremond).

28. Dan Via, "Parable and Example Story: A Literary-Structuralist Approach," *Semeia* 1 (1974) 105–33.

29. William Beardslee, "Recent Literary Criticism," 181. Similarly, Warren Kissinger, in his *The Parables of Jesus*, talks about a "rarefied atmosphere" that appears "heady and obscure" (220, 230). Beardslee also notes, however, that structuralism makes clear the multiple possibilities of meaning in any text, it clarifies the basically conflictual nature of narrative, and it raises fundamental questions about the ontological reality of narrative sense, which, in turn, would lead to the more radicalized structuralism in the "deconstruction" of Jacques Derrida (181–82).

30. As Perrin notes concerning Via's literary-structuralist analysis of the parable of the Good Samaritan (*Jesus and the Language of the Kingdom*, 180). Kissinger comments on the "minimal results" of such "prodigious efforts" (*The Parables of Jesus*, 220).

31. Noted by Perrin, *Jesus and the Language of the Kingdom*, 201.

Chapter Three: Fully Developed Literary Approaches to the Parables

1. John Dominic Crossan, *In Parable: The Challenge of the Historical Jesus* (New York: Harper & Row, 1973). The book is a rewritten collection of four previously published articles. For a much more extensive review of Crossan's works on the parables, see Frank B. Brown and Elizabeth Struthers Malbon, "Parabling as *Via Negativa*: A Critical Review of the Work of John Dominic Crossan," *Journal of Religion* 64 (1984) 530–38.

2. Crossan utilizes these terms *advent*, *reversal*, and *action* as the three categories that are basic for an understanding of all the parables and, in fact, of the entire message of Jesus. The terms are adapted from Martin Heidegger's *Being and Time*. Similarly, Crossan's "Parable is the house of God" (33) is an obvious Heideggerian allusion: "Language is the house of Being."

3. John Dominic Crossan, *The Dark Interval* (Niles, IL: Argus Communications, 1975). The quotation is from the introduction to Crossan's earlier foray into structuralist analysis, "Structuralist Analysis and the Parables of Jesus," *Semeia* 1 (1974) 192–235.

4. John Dominic Crossan, *Raid on the Articulate* (New York: Harper & Row, 1976). Cf. Robert W. Funk's *Jesus as Precursor* (Missoula, MT: Scholars Press, 1975).

5. Crossan's conception of language and the historical Jesus is conveyed even more strikingly in this book: "When I speak of Jesus I am not thinking of a personality once existent in Palestine and now in continued personal existence in heaven. By Jesus I intend…the vision and challenge of the language of Jesus…I would question whether the Lordship of Jesus derives from the permanence of his personality in heaven or from the continuance of his persona in language" (178). Crossan later joined the Jesus Seminar and published several books concerning the historical Jesus, including: *The Historical Jesus: The Life of a Mediterranean Peasant* (New York: HarperCollins, 1991); *Jesus: A Revolutionary Biography* (New York: HarperCollins, 1994); *Who Killed Jesus?* (New York: HarperCollins, 1995).

6. John Dominic Crossan, *Finding is the First Act* (Philadelphia: Fortress, 1979).

7. It is no accident that Crossan mentions the parables of Kafka on this very page! See the parable by Kafka that Crossan quotes in *Raid on the Articulate* (123–24) and compare it to the ending of Kafka's "On Parables" that Crossan cites (*In Parables*, xiv): "If you had only followed the parables you yourselves would become parables and with that rid of all your daily cares. Another said: I bet that is a parable. The first said: You have won. The second said: But unfortunately only in parable. The first said: No, in reality; in parable you have lost."

8. John Dominic Crossan, *Cliffs of Fall: Paradox and Polyvalence in the Parables of Jesus* (New York: Seabury, 1980).

9. Brown and Malbon, "Parabling as a *Via Negativa*," 534. They also wonder whether Crossan turns Jesus into a "first-century structuralist/deconstructionist" and state: "Crossan's concern to establish an authentic Jesus corpus is oddly inconsistent with the poststructuralist literary criticism on which he has increasingly relied" (536).

10. Thomas McLaughlin, "Introduction," in *Critical Terms for Literary Study*, ed. Frank Lentricchia and Thomas McLaughlin (Chicago: The University of Chicago Press, 1990), 6.

11. The work of social-scientific scholars (see chapter 6 below) and the later work of Bernard Brandon Scott would begin to address these issues. Crossan himself would incorporate some of these ideas in his book, *The Historical Jesus*.

12. Bernard Brandon Scott, *Jesus, Symbol-Maker for the Kingdom* (Philadelphia: Fortress Press, 1981).

13. The five theses are: (1) The comic appears under the guise of tragedy; (2) Grace comes to those who have no other alternative; (3) In the World of the parable the secular and religious are congruous; (4) The World of the hearer is questioned by the World of parable; (5) Faith appears as the ability to trust the depiction of World in the parable.

14. Bernard Brandon Scott, *Hear Then the Parable: A Commentary on the Parables of Jesus* (Minneapolis: Fortress Press, 1989).

15. As Crossan (*Raid on the Articulate*, 98–99), Scott describes the parables as "antimyth" because they disorder the mythical world in a world-shattering fashion (39). For a discussion of *mashal*, see chapter 4 below.

16. The "originating structure" exists at the level of *langue* and contains those features that account for subsequent performances

(*parole*) of the parable's structure. It is not a search for the actual words (*ipsissima verba*) of the historical Jesus.

17. Here Scott also affirmingly quotes Wolfgang Iser: "The implied reader designates a network of response-inviting structures, which impel the reader to grasp the text" (75). In this way, Scott hopes to encounter the "phenomenological world" reflected in the text—first-century Palestine—which forms part of the nexus in which the narrative operates, as well as informing the repertoire, conventions, worldview, ideologies, and stereotypes active in a text (76).

18. As Jeremias before him, Scott also assumes that the "expected triad" was priest, Levite, and Israelite (or "layman"; 198).

19. John Drury, *The Parables in the Gospels: History and Allegory* (New York: Crossroads, 1985). He dedicates his book "for those who are not content with the status quo in gospel criticism." Already in 1979, Mary Ann Tolbert had considered the pros and cons concerning whether parables should be interpreted in their gospel contexts in light of their polyvalency (*Perspectives on the Parables*, 51–66). The pros included having an "actual text" as a context instead of a postulated historical setting in the ministry of the historical Jesus, and a canonical context instead of one invented by the scholar. The cons included the fact that parables appear in different settings in different gospels, many of which do not "fit" the embedded parable. She finally decided that polyvalency was necessary so that the Christian community today could relate scripture to its contemporary concerns (62). Tolbert takes a different approach in her book *Sowing the Gospel* (Minneapolis: Fortress Press, 1989), in which she analyzes the parables as *parables of the gospels*, not as *parables of Jesus* (128).

20. Robert C. Tannehill, *The Narrative Unity of Luke-Acts: A Literary Interpretation*, vol. 1 (Philadelphia: Fortress Press, 1986). Cf. Mikeal C. Parsons and Richard I. Pervo, *Rethinking the Unity of Luke and Acts* (Minneapolis: Fortress Press, 1993).

21. See Ched Myers, *Binding the Strong Man* (Maryknoll, NY: Orbis, 1988). Cf. especially pages 169–74. For an similar view, but from a much different perspective, see Birger Gerhardsson, "If We Do Not Cut the Parables out of Their Frames," *New Testament Studies* 37 (1991) 321–35. Cf. Charles Talbert's treatment of the parable of the Good Samaritan in *Reading Luke* (New York: Crossroad, 1982), 122–24.

22. David B. Gowler, *Host, Guest, Enemy, and Friend: Portraits of the Pharisees in Luke and Acts* (New York, Bern, Frankfurt, Paris:

Peter Lang Press, 1991). See also David B. Gowler, "Hospitality and Characterization in Luke 11:37–54: A Socio-Narratological Approach," *Semeia* 64 (1993) 213–51.

23. In literary terms, this relation, a *mise en abyme*, is established between the "hypodiegetic" level (of the parable) and "diegetic" level (of the greater narrative) by means of an analogy (251).

24. John R. Donahue, *The Gospel as Parable* (Philadelphia: Fortress Press, 1988).

25. For a literary-critical assessment of the parables in Luke pre-dating Donahue's book, see Timothy Noël, "Parables in Context: Developing a Narrative-Critical Approach to Parables in Luke," Ph.D. dissertation, Louisville, KY: The Southern Baptist Theological Seminary, 1986.

26. Warren Carter and John Paul Heil, *Matthew's Parables*. The Catholic Biblical Quarterly Monograph Series 30 (Washington, DC: The Catholic Biblical Association of America, 1998).

27. Carter and Heil make an important distinction between the "authorial audience" (their construct of the audience the author has "in mind") and the "actual audience" (the audiences who actually read the work). Actual audiences, of course, do not always respond positively or actively to the role envisioned for them by the author (210–14).

28. This "rejoinder" is a simplistic version of my "Bakhtinian" perspective on the nature of the parables. See Mikhail Bakhtin, "The Problem of the Text," in *Speech Genres and Other Late Essays* (Austin: University of Texas Press, 1986), 103–31.

29. As W. C. Smith argues, "Scripture" is in actuality a dialogue between the text, the interpreter, and the divine: *What Is Scripture* (Minneapolis: Fortress, 1993).

30. Charles Hedrick notes: "The problem encountered in the study of parables is not unique to parables' study; it is endemic to language itself. Language, all language, is subject to ambiguity and a potential range of meanings—including even language that aims at clarity." See his *Parables as Poetic Fictions* (Peabody, MA: Hendrickson, 1994), 29. I would add, however, that some language tends to be more dialogic, and some language tends to be more monologic.

Chapter Four: The Parables and Their Jewish Contexts

1. Some recent works include, for example: John Dominic Crossan, *The Historical Jesus: The Life of a Mediterranean Jewish Peasant* (San Francisco: Harper, 1991); John P. Meier, *A Marginal Jew: Rethinking the Historical Jesus*, 2 vols. (New York: Doubleday, 1991; 1994); *The Five Gospels: The Search for the Authentic Words of Jesus*, ed. Robert W. Funk and Roy W. Hoover (New York: Macmillan, 1993); Marcus J. Borg, *Jesus: A New Vision* (San Francisco: Harper & Row, 1987); E. P. Sanders, *Jesus and Judaism* (Philadelphia: Fortress Press, 1985) and his *The Historical Figure of Jesus* (London: Penguin Press, 1993). See Gerd Theissen and Annette Merz, *The Historical Jesus: A Comprehensive Guide* (Philadelphia: Fortress, 1998).

2. See John S. Kloppenborg, ed., *The Shape of Q: Signal Sayings on the Sayings Gospel* (Minneapolis: Fortress Press, 1994); Burton L. Mack, *The Lost Gospel: The Book of Q and Christian Origins* (San Francisco: Harper, 1993); Arland D. Jacobson, *The First Gospel: An Introduction to Q* (Sonoma, CA: Polebridge, 1992).

3. See the classic statement of this problem in Henry J. Cadbury, *The Peril of Modernizing Jesus* (New York: Macmillan, 1937). These difficulties also reverberate into other areas of parable study, such as Jesus' conception of the kingdom of God and the metaphorical/allegorical elements in parables (see chapter 7 below).

4. It is generally agreed that Jesus' *lingua franca* was Aramaic. See, for example, Gustav Dalman, *Jesus-Jeshua: Studies in the Gospels*, trans. P. Levertoff (London: SPCK, 1929); Matthew Black, *An Aramaic Approach to the Gospels and Acts*, 3rd ed. (Oxford: Clarendon Press, 1967); Joachim Jeremias, *New Testament Theology: Part 1: The Proclamation of Jesus* (London: SCM, 1971). For the view that Jesus spoke the parables in Hebrew, see David Flusser and Brad Young (see below). For the view that Jesus sometimes taught in Greek, see Robert Funk and Stanley Porter (chapter 5 below). Note also the various positions held in the essays contained in *The Language of the New Testament: Classic Essays*, ed. Stanley Porter, JSNTSS 60 (Sheffield: JSOT Press, 1991). In view of the evidence, however, it seems likely that Jesus spoke Aramaic primarily, with perhaps a smattering of Greek and Hebrew.

5. Francis Brown, S. R. Driver, and Charles Briggs, *Hebrew and English Lexicon of the Old Testament* (Oxford: Clarendon Press, 1907), 695.

6. The following is compiled primarily from *The New Brown, Driver, Briggs, Gesenius Hebrew and English Lexicon*, Francis Brown, ed. Lafayette, IN: Associated Publishers and Authors, 1978), 605; L. E. Siverns, "A Definition of Parable," *Theological Review* 9 (1988) 60–75; John Drury, "Origins of Mark's Parables," in *Ways of Reading the Bible*, ed. M. Wadsworth (Brighton, Sussex: Harvester Press, 1981), 171–89.

7. John Drury separates these two examples of *mashal* by labeling 1 Sm 24:13 as a type of "popular or commonplace saying," whereas 1 Sm 10:12 is a "popular saying in figurative or comparative form" (174).

8. The NRSV here translates *mashal* as "oracle"; the Jerusalem Bible translates it as "poem."

9. Since most *meshalim* of this type are found in the prophetic writings, Siverns includes them in his "Prophetic Figurative Discourse" category (61). Bernard Brandon Scott also notes that the Septuagint prefers not to use the term *parabolē* for these taunts, an indication of its reticence to use *parabolē* in a negative sense. See his *Hear Then the Parable: A Commentary on the Parables of Jesus* (Minneapolis: Fortress Press, 1989), 20.

10. George Landes, "Jonah: A Māšāl?" in *Israelite Wisdom*, ed. J. G. Gammie (Missoula, MT: Scholars Press, 1978), 137–58.

11. *Hear Then the Parable*, 8.

12. Scott's restriction of *parabolē* to a "short narrative fiction" is critical to his conclusion because the New Testament itself uses *parabolē* in many different ways, for example as: simile (Mt 13:33), figure of speech (Mk 4:33), example (Lk 12:5–21), riddle (Mk 7:15–17), proverb (Lk 4:23), and maxim (Lk 14:7–11). In addition, Scott's use of *parable*, not surprisingly, is governed/delimited by the form in which it is found in the New Testament.

13. As the unambiguous titles of his article and essay make clear: (1) "The Narrative Meshalim in the Synoptic Gospels: A Comparison with the Narrative Meshalim in the Old Testament," *NTS* 34 (1988) 339–63; (2) "The Narrative Meshalim in the Old Testament Books and in the Synoptic Gospels," in *To Touch the Text*, ed. M. Horgan and P. Kobelski (New York: Crossroad, 1989), 289–304.

14. Similarly in Michael Goulder, *Midrash and Lection in Matthew* (London: SPCK, 1974), 47.

15. For another comparison of the uses of parable, simile, metaphor, and allegory in both the Hebrew Bible and the gospels, see Claus Westermann, *The Parables of Jesus in Light of the Old Testament* (Minneapolis: Fortress, 1990).

16. In this section, I am dependent on the expertise of Lawrence Boadt, "Understanding the *Mashal* and Its Value for the Jewish-Christian Dialogue in a Narrative Theology," in *Parable and Story in Judaism and Christianity*, ed. Clemens Thoma and Michael Wyschogrod (Mahwah, NJ: Paulist Press: 1989), 159–88.

17. David W. Suter, "Māšāl in the Similitudes of Enoch," *JBL* 100 (1981) 197.

18. Timothy Polk, "Paradigms, Parables, and *Měšālîm*: On Reading the Māšāl in Scripture," *CBQ* 45 (1983) 565. Polk also commended Landes for his concentration on content and function, not type or form (566).

19. Examples of such polemics are, sadly, easy to find: (1) "The [rabbinic] parables are designed to illustrate the distorted ideas of a dead learning…"; Wilhelm Bouset, *Jesus*, trans. Janet Penrose Trevelyan (London: Williams & Norgate, 1906); David Stern illustrates this problem with Adolph Jülicher's opinion that Jesus' parables were "fresh as the air of the Galilean mountains," but that the rabbinic parables were characterized as "pedantic, forced, and artificial," in "Jesus' Parables from the Perspective of Rabbinic Literature: The Example of the Wicked Husbandmen," in *Parable and Story in Judaism and Christianity*, 42–43. The "uniqueness" and/or "superiority" of Jesus' parables was a standard position among most Christian scholars. As Craig Blomberg correctly notes, however, a "more careful reading" of Tannaitic parables, for example, refutes such a misinformed bias (*Interpreting the Parables* [Downers Grove, IL.: IVP, 1990], 58) (n.b., the *Tannaitic* period is roughly the period from the beginning of the Christian era to around 220 C.E. when Rabbi Judah ha-Nasi completed the document known as the Mishnah—the early rabbinical commentary on the Torah).

This assessment is even more interesting when one notes the work of Theodor Guttmann, who claimed that: (1) the parables of Jesus and the Rabbis are basically the same genre, and (2) the *Tannaitic* parables are superior to later rabbinical parables (*Ha-mashal bikufat ha-tannaim*

[*The Parable in the Tannaitic Period*] [Jerusalem: "Guild" Cooperative Press, 1940]) (I am indebted to the English summary found in Harvey K. McArthur and Robert M. Johnston, *They Also Taught in Parables* [Grand Rapids: Zondervan, 1990], 204–5). The point is that not all rabbinic parables were created equal!

20. Israel Abrahams, *Studies in Pharisaism and the Gospels* (London: Cambridge University Press, 1917).

21. Asher Feldman, *The Parables and Similies of the Rabbis* (Cambridge: Cambridge University Press, 1927). Feldman's work is a valuable collation of rabbinic texts of similes, metaphors, allegories, parables, proverbs, and other similar materials.

22. Christian A. Bugge, *Die Haupt-Parabeln Jesu* (Giessen: J. Rickerische Verlagsbuchhandlung, 1903); Paul Fiebig, *Altjüdische Gleichnisse und die Gleichnisse Jesu* (Tübingen: J. C. B. Mohr, 1904); Paul Fiebig, *Die Gleichnisreden Jesu im Lichte der rabbinischen Gleichnisse des neutestamentlichen Zeitalters* (Tübingen: J. C. B. Mohr, 1912). For (English) summaries and analysis, see Warren S. Kissinger, *The Parables of Jesus: A History of Interpretation and Bibliography* (Metuchen, NJ: The Scarecrow Press, 1979), 77–83; and McArthur and Johnson, *They Also Taught in Parables*, 203.

23. Cf. McArthur and Johnson, *They Also Taught in Parables*, 203–4. His analysis also opened the way for allegorical elements to be "readmitted in the front door" (i.e., that Jülicher's distinction between allegory and parable was overdrawn).

24. One such effort involves the team of Clemens Thoma (a Christian scholar) and Simon Lauer (a Jewish scholar). They are attempting to edit, translate, analyze, and comment on "*all* of the rabbinic parables" (approximately 1300!) to shed light on the various contexts—literary, historical, and theological—of these parables.

25. Clemens Thoma, "Literary and Theological Aspects of the Rabbinic Parables," in *Parable and Story in Judaism and Christianity*, 27.

26. As noted by Lawrence Boadt, "Understanding the *Mashal*," 167.

27. *Deuteronomy Rabbah* is a rather late midrash on Deuteronomy (ninth or tenth century) that is part of the *Midrash Rabbah Series*. The parable may be found in *They Also Taught in Parables*, 83 (noted above).

28. For some of these arguments from quite diverse (Christian) perspectives, see Scott, *Hear Then the Parable*, 8–19, and Craig Blomberg, *Interpreting the Parables*, 65–69.

29. David Flusser, *Jewish Sources in Early Christianity* (Tel-Aviv: MOD Books, 1989), 11–12. Flusser also holds the idiosyncratic view that the "original Gospels" were written in "Rabbinic Hebrew." Flusser's primary book on the parables has not been translated into English (*Die rabbinischen Gleichnisse und der Gleichniserzähler Jesus* [Bern: Peter Lang, 1981]). Because its influence is also felt, in varying degrees, through two of his former students (David Stern and Brad Young), I will briefly summarize his conclusions.

30. For a brief English statement of this position, see his "Aesop's Miser and the Parable of the Talents," in *Parable and Story in Judaism and Christianity*, 9–25.

31. His Hebrew University (Jerusalem) dissertation was revised and published as *Jesus and His Jewish Parables: Rediscovering the Roots of Jesus' Teaching* (Mahwah, NJ: Paulist Press, 1989).

32. Philip L. Culbertson, *A Word Fitly Spoken* (Albany: SUNY Press, 1995), xiii, 8–9.

33. *Halakhah* is legal material; *midrash* is the "method by which any text is hermeneutically reinterpreted to draw forth an explanation of an inner meaning of that text" (69). Using the rabbinic contexts and "listener-response theory," Culbertson provides interpretations of six Matthean parables.

34. "The Rabbinic Parable: From Rhetoric to Poetics," in *The Society of Biblical Literature Seminar Papers* 25 (Atlanta: Scholars Press, 1986), 631–43; "Jesus' Parables from the Perspective of Rabbinic Literature: The Example of the Wicked Husbandman," in *Parable and Story in Judaism and Christianity*, 42–80; *Parables and Midrash* (Cambridge: Harvard University Press, 1991).

35. It should be noted that this "full maturity" includes a "state of almost complete stereotyping" (43). Stern's later revision of this phrase to "more comprehensively preserved" is a necessary clarification. Stern is also aware of the difficulties inherent in reconstructing this trajectory, such as: (1) utilizing rabbinic parables from a period nearly two and a half centuries after the time of Jesus makes one extremely susceptible to anachronism; (2) the difficulty of recovering the "original" sayings of Jesus; (3) the difficulty of recovering the "original" sayings of the rabbis

quoted in rabbinic literature (43). To sidestep the latter two problems, Stern argues that "the only viable comparison…is between the texts of Jesus' parables *as preserved by the editors/authors of the synoptic gospels* and the *meshalim* of the Rabbis *as preserved by the editors/ authors of the Rabbinic literary collections*" (emphasis his; 1989:45).

In *Parables in Midrash*, Stern adds some other caveats. (4) the parables of Jesus are not preserved in their original language; (5) because of #2 and #3 above, the problems become multiplied when the two types of texts are compared.

36. This duplication can act as a safeguard, in effect providing buoys in the channel of interpretation. Stern also argues that by introducing differences between the *mashal* and the *nimshal*, the message could be deliberately complicated by "additional subtleties" (1991:9).

37. Noted by Boadt, "Understanding the *Mashal*," 171–72. A further critique was offered by Anthony Saldarini: "Stern does show how parables work in their midrashic contexts, but stops before facing the full philosophical, literary, and theological complexities of narrative, language, and interpretation." See Anthony J. Saldarini, "David Stern, *Parables in Midrash: Narrative and Exegesis in Rabbinic Literature*," in *Religious Studies Review* 22:2 (1996) 120.

Chapter Five: The Parables and Their Hellenistic Contexts

1. See the forceful arguments in Vernon K. Robbins, "Interpreting the Gospel of Mark as a Jewish Document in a Greco-Roman World," in *New Boundaries in Old Territory: Form and Social Rhetoric in Mark*, ed. David B. Gowler (New York: Peter Lang, 1994), 219–42.

2. Funk originally made this proposal in "The Narrative Parables: The Birth of a Language Tradition," *St. Andrews Review* (Spring-Summer 1974) 299–323. It reappeared in a 1977 book of essays, *God's Christ and his People*, ed. J. Jervell and W. Meeks (Oslo: Univeritetsforlaget, 1977), 43–50. It may also be found in Funk's *Parables and Presence* (Philadelphia: Fortress Press, 1982), 19–28.

3. In contrast, T. W. Manson claims that "The detection of rhythm in our Lord's utterances depends to a large extent on retranslation into Aramaic." See his *The Teaching of Jesus: Studies in Form and*

Content (Cambridge: Cambridge University Press, 1931; 2nd ed. rpt. 1951), 53.

4. Funk concludes that this could have come from Jesus primarily but not necessarily. It also could have come from "some other" during the early stages of the Christian tradition (1977:50).

5. Stanley Porter, for example, defends Jesus' teaching competence in Greek without referring to Funk's work. See his "Did Jesus Ever Teach in Greek?" *Tyndale Bulletin* 44 (1993) 199–235.

6. Charles Hedrick, *Parables as Poetic Fictions: The Creative Voice of Jesus* (Peabody, MA: Hendrickson, 1994).

7. Hedrick does not make this explicit, but this difference would still hold true even if the parables were initially spoken in Greek, but it is even more true if Jesus composed them originally in Aramaic. The Greek parables would have to be extensively reworked from Aramaic to produce such euphony in their present Greek form.

8. Adolph Jülicher, *Die Gleichnisreden Jesu* (Tübingen: Mohr-Siebeck, 1899), I.98.

9. *The Teaching of Jesus*, 57–58.

10. Madeline Boucher, *The Mysterious Parable: A Literary Study*. The Catholic Quarterly Monograph Series 6 (Washington, DC: The Catholic Biblical Association of America, 1977), 13.

11. Theon's quote is from *Progymnasmata* 3. Perry's endorsement is made in his "Introduction" to *Babrius and Phaedrus*, Loeb Classical Library (Cambridge: Harvard University Press, 1965), xxiii. Cited by Mary Ann Beavis, "Parable and Fable," *CBQ* 52 (1990) 476.

12. "Introduction" to *Babrius and Phaedrus*, xxviii–xxxiv. Also cited by Beavis with corroborative arguments (478).

13. *Paideia* was used regularly to denote both teaching and culture in Hellenistic-Roman societies.

14. "Lazarus and Micyllus: Greco-Roman Backgrounds to Luke 16:19–31," *JBL* 106 (1987) 447–63.

15. Hock correctly recognizes that the reasons are primarily theological (i.e., Jesus' teaching as unique and "unaffected" by its Hellenistic-Roman milieu and superior to its Jewish context), sociological (i.e., the belief that a poor, rural, Galilean carpenter would not have had much contact with the Hellenistic-Roman culture; N.B., the Hellenistic city Sepphoris was just six miles from Nazareth!), and disciplinary (i.e.,

New Testament scholars no longer have much classical training in the broader Hellenistic-Roman contexts).

16. Richard Bauckham responds that Hock was correct in suggesting that the Hellenistic texts were *also* relevant, but incorrect to suggest that they were *more* relevant than the Egyptian story. See his "The Rich Man and Lazarus: The Parable and the Parallels" *NTS* 37 (1991) 225–46. Bauckham's point may be stressed as a general rule: Attention should be given to all available comparative texts, and the similarities *and* differences should be examined closely (cf. 246).

17. F. G. Downing, *Cynics and Christian Origins* (Edinburgh: T & T Clark, 1992), 139.

18. For examples of a more full analysis of specific references in Q and their correspondence to Cynic materials, see F. G. Downing, *Christ and the Cynics* (Sheffield: Sheffield University Press, 1988); and Leif E. Vaage, *Galilean Upstarts: Jesus' First Followers According to Q* (Valley Forge: Trinity Press, 1994).

19. If I may belabor the metaphor, his words have often fallen on rocky ground. Burton L. Mack, *A Myth of Innocence: Mark and Christian Origins* (Philadelphia: Fortress Press, 1988); Burton L. Mack and Vernon K. Robbins, *Patterns of Persuasion in the Gospels* (Sonoma, CA: Polebridge Press, 1989), 143–60. I will only discuss aspects that specifically pertain to the comparison of the parables in Mark 4:1–34 with Hellenistic-Roman texts.

20. Mack cites four texts in particular (1988:159–60). I will reproduce two of them:

"As is the seed that is ploughed into the ground, so must one expect the harvest to be, and similarly when good education is ploughed into your persons, its effect lives and burgeons throughout their lives, and neither rain nor drought can destroy it" (Antiphon).

"Words should be scattered like seed; no matter how small the seed may be, if it once has found favorable ground, it unfolds its strength and from an insignificant thing spreads to its greatest growth" (Seneca, *Epistles* 38:2).

21. "Interpreting Miracle Culture and Parable Culture in Mark 4–11," *Svensk Exegetisk Årsbok* 59 (1994) 59–81.

22. Willi Braun, *Feasting and Social Rhetoric in Luke 14* (Cambridge: Cambridge University Press, 1995).

23. The Pharisees in Luke should not be confused with the historical Pharisees. Luke's Gospel, to a large extent, presents a caricature of the Pharisees, which includes a range of four basic responses to Jesus and his followers. See the analyses in David B. Gowler, *Host, Guest, Enemy, and Friend: Portraits of the Pharisees in Luke and Acts*, Emory Studies in Early Christianity 1 (New York, Paris, Bern: Peter Lang Press, 1991), and "Hospitality and Characterization in Luke 11:37–54: A Socio-Narratological Approach," *Semeia* 64 (1994) 213–51.

24. What Braun does not mention is that this peer exclusion is a classic example of *hubris*, the deliberate infliction of dishonor and shame upon another. The insults of the host by the invited guests were thus grievous assaults on his person or honor. See my review of Braun's book in *Toronto Journal of Theology* 13/1 (1997) 97–98.

25. As noted by Mikhail M. Bakhtin, *The Dialogic Imagination,* ed. Michael Holquist (Austin: University of Texas Press, 1981), 64. On the next page is a scientific analogy that in the context of the present book turns into a pun: "Where languages and cultures interanimated each other, language became something entirely different, its very nature changed: in place of a single unitary sealed-off Ptolemaic world of language, there appeared the open Galilean world of many languages, mutually animating each other" (65).

Chapter Six: The Parables and Their Social Contexts

1. For cogent analyses of this development, see Carolyn Osiek, *What Are They Saying About the Social Setting of the New Testament?,* rev. ed. (Mahwah, NJ: Paulist Press, 1992); and John H. Elliott, *What Is Social-Scientific Criticism?* (Minneapolis: Fortress Press, 1993).

2. Kenneth E. Bailey, *Poet and Peasant: A Literary-Cultural Approach to the Parables in Luke* (Grand Rapids, MI: Eerdmans, 1976). See also his *Through Peasant Eyes* (Grand Rapids, MI: Eerdmans, 1980).

3. Like Joachim Jeremias, Bailey had lived in the Middle East and was able to incorporate many cultural insights in his work. A comparison of their interpretations of the Good Samaritan (*Through Peasant Eyes*, 33–56) finds many similarities (e.g., the assumption that an

ancient hearer would have expected an Israelite layperson to be the third person coming down the road; 47).

4. As noted by William R. Herzog, *Parables as Subversive Speech* (Louisville, KY: W/JKP, 1994), 54.

5. The necessity of clarifying these ideological boundaries is made clear by Vernon K. Robbins in his *Jesus the Teacher*, rev. ed. (Philadelphia: Fortress Press, 1992), xxxviii. Such methodological ambiguity spills over into Bailey's literary analyses. It is not clear, for example, whether he is more concerned about the parables' literary audience (e.g., *Poet*, 87, 108) or the historical audience (e.g., *Poet*, 139–41).

6. Bernard Brandon Scott, *Hear Then the Parable* (Minneapolis: Fortress Press, 1989).

7. The first group of parables focuses on aspects of social relations. Social exchanges were organized around the family as the central social unit, and social organization moved out in concentric circles from the family unit. These artifacts of daily life were often used to symbolize the larger transcendent values of life. The second group of parables embodies the model of patron-client relationships as organizations of power exchanges, which, in Jesus' parables, usually involve a test between master and servant. The third group of parables invests the artifacts of daily life with "metaphorical and symbolic significance" (73–74).

8. The term comes from Paulo Freire, a modern Brazilian educator (16–29). Herzog's brief critique of the facade of an "objective observer" is one of the most cogent I have read (15–16). Thus Herzog brings his own ideological perspective into the open, a move that should be applauded and emulated, even if one does not agree with his perspective or his interpretations of specific parables.

9. For males, shame is a negative value that involves the loss of honor. For females, however, shame is a positive value of sensitivity to and defense of honor. The literature is vast, but see especially, J. G. Peristiany, ed., *Honour and Shame: The Values of Mediterranean Society* (Chicago: University of Chicago Press, 1966); J. G. Peristiany and Julian Pitt-Rivers, eds., *Honour and Grace in Mediterranean Society* (Cambridge: Cambridge University Press, 1991); Frank Henderson Stewart, *Honor* (Chicago: The University of Chicago Press, 1994). For applications to New Testament studies, see, for example, Bruce Malina

and Jerry Neyrey, "Honor and Shame in Luke-Acts: Pivotal Values of the Mediterranean World," in Jerry Neyrey, ed., *The Social World of Luke-Acts* (Peabody, MA: Hendrickson, 1991), 25–65.

10.   Carolyn Osiek, *Social Setting*, 26.

11.   "Ascribed honor," on the other hand, is derived from birth or inheritance, and it situates you into your appropriate place in the social hierarchy.

12.   What Malina and Neyrey do not make explicit are the additional reasons the lawyer is shamed. Not only does he lose the honor/shame contest, it becomes clear to the people standing around that because the lawyer already knew the answer (10:27), he was only trying to put Jesus to the test—something the narrator already made clear to the readers (10:25).

13.   Herzog, *Parables as Subversive Speech*, 79–97. For a critique of Herzog's analysis, see V. George Shillington, "Saving Life and Keeping Sabbath (Matthew 20:1b–15)," in *Jesus and His Parables*, ed. V. George Shillington (Edinburgh: T & T Clark, 1997), 87–101. Shillington argues that Herzog pays too little attention to the subjects in the parable who did not have a full day's wage. Shillington thus has a more positive view of the landowner who "learned from his trip to the marketplace at the end of the day that gross inequality of life exists between worker and worker, and between the workers and himself" (98). One wonders, however, if Shillington has accurately gauged just how new and shocking this information would be to a first-century landowner. Cf. Herzog's statement about the elite "despising" peasants (69).

14.   Herzog notes that the "excess" children (i.e., those who cannot be fed) of peasant farmers and others constitute members of the "expendables." The percentage of expendables ranged from 5 percent to 15 percent of the population. The elites in the ancient world squeezed the dwindling resources of the peasants through taxation and other forms of redistribution, so these persons were forced into the most degrading and lethal form of poverty. Herzog estimates that they typically lived no more than five to seven years after entering this class, but many more came to take the place of those who died (65–66).

15.   John H. Elliott, "Matthew 20:1–15: A Parable of Invidious Comparison and Evil Eye Accusation," *BTB* 22 (1992) 52–65.

16. For succinct definitions of *emic* and *etic*, see Elliott, *What is Social-Scientific Criticism?*, 129. No modern interpreter, of course, can truly take a fully emic perspective.

17. This chapter title is a reference to Henry J. Cadbury's important critique of interpreters' anachronizing tendencies in *The Peril of Modernizing Jesus* (London: Macmillan, 1937).

18. Halvor Moxnes, "Patron–Client Relations and the New Community in Luke-Acts," in *The Social World of Luke-Acts*, 241–68.

19. Douglas E. Oakman, *Jesus and the Economic Questions of His Day* (Lewiston, NY: Edwin Mellen, 1986). See also his "The Ancient Economy in the Bible," *BTB* 21 (1991) 34–39.

20. An elite, on the other hand, would consider such labor as shameful.

21. Oakman cites several sources (176–93) that seem to indicate that Jesus, before his public ministry, would have been under great pressure to travel to nearby urban areas, such as Sepphoris or Tiberias, to find enough work to provide for his family (i.e., mother and siblings).

22. Douglas E. Oakman, "Was Jesus a Peasant?: Implications for Reading the Samaritan Story (Luke 10:30–35)," *BTB* 22 (1992) 117–25.

23. Douglas E. Oakman, "The Countryside in Luke-Acts," in *The Social World of Luke-Acts*, 151–79.

24. Richard L. Rohrbaugh, "A Peasant Reading of the Parable of the Talents/Pounds: A Text of Terror?," *BTB* 23 (1993) 32–39.

25. See also Rohrbaugh's intriguing reading of the Prodigal Son in his "A Dysfunctional Family and Its Neighbors (Luke 15:11b–32)" found in the collection of various essays in *Jesus and His Parables* (141–64). Rohrbaugh envisions this parable, as he does many parables of Jesus, as a story where people break all the conventional rules of honor: A foolish father divides his estate while alive, runs to rescue a shameless son, and begs another son bent on humiliating him in public. Because of peasant society's exaltation of social conformity, the well-being and future of the entire extended family is at stake.

26. Noted by Nicola Slee, "Parables and Women's Experiences," *Religious Education* 80 (1985) 232–45. Domestic affairs are also rarely mentioned.

27. John H. Elliott, "Temple Versus Household in Luke-Acts: A Contrast in Social Institutions," in *The Social World of Luke-Acts*, 211–40.

28. Stuart L. Love, "The Household: A Major Social Component for Gender Analysis in the Gospel of Matthew," *BTB* 23 (1993) 21–31.

29. Stuart L. Love, "The Place of Women in Public Settings in Matthew's Gospel: A Sociological Inquiry," *BTB* 24 (1994) 52–65.

30. Alicia Batten, "More Queries for Q: Women and Christian Origins," *BTB* 24 (1994) 44–51.

31. The Q community was not unique in this inclusion (e.g., other groups such as the Jewish *Therapeutae* were similar in this regard), but it is unusual.

32. Carol Schersten LaHurd, "Rediscovering the Lost Women in Luke 15," *BTB* 24 (1994) 66–76.

33. Women have "informal power," but LaHurd agrees with Kathleen Corley that their power was ultimately derivative in nature and more a matter of influence rather than direct control (71). See Kathleen Corley, *Private Women, Public Meals* (Peabody, MA: Hendrickson, 1993), 454–56. LaHurd concludes, however, that the parables of Luke 15 bring together both public and private, male and female realms into one narrative of celebration.

34. Diane Jacobs-Malina, *Beyond Patriarchy* (Mahwah, NJ: Paulist, 1993).

35. See the categorization of the four basic approaches to women and the New Testament in scholarship by Carolyn Osiek in "The Feminist and the Bible: Hermeneutical Alternatives," in *Feminist Perspectives on Biblical Scholarship*, ed. Adela Yarbro Collins (Chico, CA: Scholars Press, 1985), 93–105.

36. See Jacobs-Malina, *Beyond Patriarchy,* 9.

37. Elizabeth Schüssler-Fiorenza, *In Memory of Her: A Feminist Theological Reconstruction of Christian Origins* (New York: Crossroads, 1989), 151.

Chapter Seven: From Simile and Metaphor to Symbol and Emblematic Language

1. See the discussion of Funk's work (and the other references cited in that discussion) in chapter 2 above.

2. Norman Perrin, *The Kingdom of God in the Teaching of Jesus* (London: SCM Press, 1963) and *Jesus and the Language of the Kingdom* (Philadelphia: Fortress Press, 1976).

3. See the discussions in Norman Perrin, *Jesus and the Language of the Kingdom,* 34–40; John K. Riches, *A Century of New Testament Study* (Valley Forge, PA: Trinity Press, 1993), 14–30; Wendell Willis, "The Discovery of the Eschatological Kingdom: Johannes Weiss and Albert Schweitzer," in *The Kingdom of God in 20th Century Interpretation,* ed. Wendell Willis (Peabody, MA: Hendrickson Press, 1987), 1–14. Gösta Lundström (*The Kingdom of God in the Teaching of Jesus* [Richmond: John Knox, 1963]) notes that Ritschl and his students were primarily responsible for establishing the kingdom of God as the primary focus of theology in the nineteenth century.

4. As many observers have noted, this idea was greatly indebted to the ethical idealism of Immanuel Kant.

5. See Riches, *New Testament Study,* 15–16.

6. For a critique of this common opinion in connection with the parables, see Charles Hedrick, *Parables as Poetic Fictions* (Peabody, MA: Hendrickson, 1994): "In my judgment, the varieties of understanding of the 'kingdom' within early Christianity demonstrate that it was a problem, and that problem provides a plausible historical context for the association of the stories of Jesus with the kingdom of God. This explanation is at least as plausible as the argument that the historical Jesus himself associated his stories with the kingdom" (77).

7. The much longer second edition of 1900 has been published as *Jesus' Proclamation of the Kingdom of God,* ed. and trans. R. H. Hiers and D. L. Holland (Philadelphia: Fortress Press, 1971). For a thorough discussion of the contributions of Weiss, Albert Schweitzer, Martin Dibelius, Rudolph Bultmann, and others, see Warren Kissinger, *The Parables of Jesus* (Metuchen, NJ: Scarecrow Press, 1979), 89–117.

8. See the discussion of Norman Perrin, *Jesus and the Language of the Kingdom,* 34–40.

9. C. H. Dodd, *The Parables of the Kingdom,* rev. ed. (Glasgow: Collins, 1961), 29–38. The first statement of Dodd's "realized eschatology" was made in "The Other-Worldly Kingdom of God in Our Lord's Teaching," *Theology* 14 (1927) 258–60. Dodd came to prefer Jeremias's term *sich realisierenden Eschatologie* (eschatology in the process of realization), but his essential position only changed slightly. See his *The Inter-*

pretation of the Fourth Gospel (Cambridge: University Press, 1953), 447, and *The Coming of God* (Cambridge: University Press, 1951).

10. See Perrin's comments in *Jesus and the Language of the Kingdom,* 37–39.

11. Brad H. Young, *Jesus and His Jewish Parables* (New York: Paulist Press, 1989).

12. In addition, E. P. Sanders notes that almost any first-century Jew could have agreed that God rules here and now because God exercises providence and controls the ultimate outcome. In general terms that view, Sanders argues, was "completely non-controversial." See his *The Historical Figure of Jesus* (London: Penguin Press, 1993), 171. In contrast, Sanders believes that Jesus' life embodied a "Jewish restoration theology." Jesus had an eschatological message: God would intervene decisively to create an ideal world in which God would restore the twelve tribes of Israel, and peace and justice would prevail. See also his *Jesus and Judaism* (Philadelphia: Fortress Press, 1985).

13. Perrin, *Jesus and the Language of the Kingdom,* 40. He notes that the only contemporary rejection of this "partially realized eschatology" during this era of consensus was by Richard H. Hiers, *The Kingdom of God in the Synoptic Tradition* (Gainesville: University of Florida Press, 1970), who attempted to reinstate the eschatological views of Weiss.

14. Norman Perrin, *The Kingdom of God in the Teaching of Jesus.*

15. W. G. Kümmel, *Promise and Fulfillment* (London: SCM Press, 1957).

16. Aloysius Ambrozic, *The Hidden Kingdom* (Washington, DC: The Catholic Biblical Association of America, 1972).

17. George Eldon Ladd, *The Presence of the Future* (Grand Rapids, MI: Eerdmans, 1974). This work is a revision of his *Jesus and the Kingdom* (New York: Harper & Row, 1964).

18. George Beasley-Murray, *Jesus and the Future* (London: Macmillan, 1954) and his magisterial *Jesus and the Kingdom of God* (Grand Rapids, MI: Eerdmans, 1986).

19. For a treatment of all the parables that include this "here and now" aspect, see 108–46.

20. As noted by Kümmel, *Promise and Fulfillment,* 56.

21. See W. Emory Elmore, "Linguistic Approaches to the Kingdom: Amos Wilder and Norman Perrin," in *The Kingdom of God in*

20th-Century Interpretation, ed. Wendell Willis (Peabody, MA: Hendrickson, 1987), 59–65.

22. *The Kingdom of God in the Teaching of Jesus.*

23. Perrin uses *myth* to mean a complex of stories—whether "fact" or "fantasy"—that human beings regard as demonstrations of the inner meaning of the universe and human life. Perrin borrows here from both Alan Watts and Philip Wheelwright (22).

24. Perrin incorporates the work of Philip Wheelwright on "steno-symbol" and "tensive symbol," as well as the work of Paul Ricoeur on "sign" and "symbol." His literary approach to the parables was influenced by his contemporaries, Amos Wilder, Robert Funk, Dan Otto Via, and John Dominic Crossan.

25. Or, in the words of J. Hillis Miller, a parable does not so much passively name something as to make something happen. The performative word makes something happen in the minds and hearts of its hearers—it brings the kingdom of God—and, in that sense, a parable is constative, not performative. See his *Tropes, Parables, Performatives: Essays on Twentieth-Century Literature* (New York: Harvester, 1991), 139.

26. Amos Wilder, *The Language of the Gospel: Early Christian Rhetoric,* rev. ed. (New York: Harper & Row, 1971).

27. Robert W. Funk, *Language, Hermeneutic, and the Word of God* (New York: Harper & Row, 1966), 137. Funk writes in his *Honest to Jesus* (San Francisco: Harper, 1996), 168: "For [Jesus] the future was fused together with the past in the intensity of the present moment to such a degree that he did not distinguish the past, present, and future as modes of time."

28. Dan Otto Via, *The Parables: Their Literary and Existential Dimension* (Philadelphia: Fortress, 1967). In his structuralist work, Via argues that the kingdom of God is always represented, although not always expressed explicitly, by a king-master-father figure.

29. John Dominic Crossan, *In Parable: The Challenge of the Historical Jesus* (New York: Harper & Row, 1973). Crossan thus argues that the kingdom of God is neither "prophetic" or "apocalyptic" but permanent presence. A refinement of this position is found in his book *The Historical Jesus* (San Francisco: Harper, 1991). See especially the section entitled "The Brokerless Kingdom" (225–416). Crossan states, "What was described by his parables and aphorisms as a here and now kingdom of the nobodies and the destitute, of mustard, darnel, and

leaven, is precisely a kingdom performed rather than just proclaimed." Jesus was "located" within the "sapiential" and "peasant": He looked to the present rather than the future and imagined how one could live here and now within an already or always available divine dominion. It was a style of life rather than a hope in the future, although it could be just as eschatological and world negating as an apocalyptic kingdom. And, as a "peasant," Jesus "performed" the kingdom in his words and actions (292). Compare the view of Marcus J. Borg in *Jesus: A New Vision* (San Francisco: Harper & Row, 1987), 197–99.

30. Bernard Brandon Scott, *Jesus, Symbol-Maker for the Kingdom* (Philadelphia: Fortress Press, 1981).

31. Robert Hamilton, "The Gospel of Mark: Parable of God Incarnate," *Theology* 86 (1983) 438–41.

32. J. Hillis Miller, *Tropes, Parables, Performatives,* 138.

33. John R. Donahue, *The Gospel in Parable* (Philadelphia: Fortress Press, 1988). See also the warning of Mary Ann Tolbert in her *Perspectives on the Parables* (Philadelphia: Fortress Press, 1979), 42–43. Andrew Parker takes even a more pointed approach. He quotes the simile, "The cat's eyes were as black as coal," and states: "People would rightly laugh if one were to claim that there was 'an intrinsic and inalienable bond' between the experience of a cat's dilated pupils and the coal simile but the fact is that it is just as pretentious to talk about Jesus' parables in such terms." Compare his *Painfully Clear: The Parables of Jesus* (Sheffield: Sheffield Academic Press, 1996), 54, with John Dominic Crossan's *In Parables,* 22.

34. Madeleine I. Boucher, *The Parables* (Wilmington, DE: Michael Glazier, 1981).

35. This position is a needed corrective to John Sider's statement that "parable and allegory are one in form." See his "Proportional Analogy in the Gospel Parables," *New Testament Studies* 31 (1985) 1–23.

36. As Aristotle noted in his *On Style* 2.82: "No change of phrase could, by the employment of precise terms, convey the meaning with greater truth or clearness [than by a metaphor]." Quintillian classifies metaphor as "by far the most beautiful of the tropes" that is used necessarily "to make our meaning clearer" (Quintillian, *Institutio Oratoria* 8.6.4 and 8.6.6).

37. William F. Brosend II, "The Limits of Metaphor," *Perspectives in Religious Studies* 21:1 (1994) 23–41. Brosend then summarizes

the insights of Donald Davidson, Ted Cohen, and Wayne Booth from the work *On Metaphor* (ed. Sheldon Sacks [Chicago: University of Chicago, 1979]): (1) Metaphors are rhetorical, not semantic, creatures and have a persuasive, rhetorical purpose—to enhance communication; (2) This purpose, and in many instances the metaphor itself, can be readily paraphrased, although the paraphrase is not the equivalent of the metaphor; (3) The metaphor communicates more than its literal meaning, but this aspect is not additional cognitive content but is the metaphor's effect on the hearer. Rhetorically speaking, metaphors do not mean more than they say, but they do have a persuasive impact greater than a nonmetaphoric expression would have. This is not the "creation" of meaning but is rather the "communication" of meaning; (4) Finally, a metaphor's intended effect is the "cultivation of intimacy" that enhances the relationship of speaker and hearer through the shared interpretive experience created by the metaphor (41).

38. Mary Ford, "Towards the Restoration of Allegory," *Saint Vladimir's Theological Quarterly* 34 (1990) 161–95. See also John MacQueen's *Allegory* (London: Methuen, 1970). He discusses "biblical allegory" (18–36) and describes parables as primarily prophetic and situational allegories (23). Note how differently MacQueen characterizes parables (as "direct and immediate" allegories) from many biblical scholars: "...the parables were more relevant, more exciting, than even the latest political or military news. This is as true of the apparently narrative or figural allegories as of the situational" (26).

39. Hans-Josef Klauck, *Allegorie und Allegorese in synoptischen Gleichnistexten* (Munster: Aschendorff, 1978), 20, 91. See also the thoughtful comments of J. Ian H. McDonald, "Alien Grace (Luke 10:30–36)" in *Jesus and His Parables,* ed. V. George Shillington (Edinburgh: T&T Clark, 1997), 35–39. His example of the stained glass windows at Chartres interpreting the parable of the Good Samaritan for that day is helpful: "They were enlarging upon its interpretation, but not telling a different story. They were pushing the metaphor to its limits" (38). Also, on the same page: "Parable and allegory do not belong to different worlds or genres of literature. Both depend on narrative and analogy."

40. As translated by Carl Carlston in his review of Klauck's book. See *Catholic Biblical Quarterly* 43 (1981) 228–42. For another example of a scholar who accepts as authentic allegorical elements in

the parables, see Klyne Snodgrass, who asks the question, "Can a parable be an allegory?" and then answers affirmatively. See his *The Parable of the Wicked Tenants* (Tübingen: Mohr, 1983), 12–26. Compare the discussion of Graham Ward, who argues that biblical narratives should be read as both metaphor and metonymy in his "Biblical Narrative and the Theology of Metonymy," *Modern Theology* 7:4 (1991) 335–49.

41.   David B. Batstone, "Jesus, Apocalyptic, and World Transformation," *Theology Today* 49 (1992) 383–97.

42.   William Herzog, *Parables as Subversive Speech* (Louisville: Westminster/John Knox Press, 1994), 9.

43.   Herzog's social and cultural insights have been both critiqued and extended. See, for example, the essays found in *Jesus and His Parables,* ed. V. George Shillington (Edinburgh: T & T Clark, 1997). Note especially, Mary Ann Beavis, "The Foolish Landowner," 55–68, and V. George Shillington, "Saving Life and Keeping Sabbath," 87–101.

44.   See Paul Fiebig, *Altjüdische Gleichnisse und die Gleichnisse Jesu* (Tübingen: Mohr, 1904); *Die Gleichnisreden Jesu im Lichte der rabbinischen Gleichnisse des neutestamentlichen Zeitalters* (Tübingen: Mohr, 1912).

45.   Raymond Brown, "Parable and Allegory Reconsidered," *Novum Testamentum* 5 (1962) 36–45. For a creative development of this argument, see John Drury, "Origins of Mark's Parables," in *Ways of Reading the Bible,* ed. M. Wadsworth (Brighton, Sussex: Harvester Press, 1981), 171–89. Drury argues that the parables in Mark are "historical allegories" that have their origin in the *mashal* as developed in Ezekiel, Daniel, and other Jewish literature. The parables as used by Mark can be historical, allegorical, obscure, and eschatological (182–83).

46.   David Stern, *Parables and Midrash* (Cambridge: Harvard University Press, 1991), 11. Stern suggests that the opposite of metaphor is not allegory but metonymy (12). Robert Johnson concludes that the distinction between parable and allegory is "unusable." See his "Parabolic Interpretations Attributed to Tannaim" (Hartford: Ph.D. thesis, 1978), 636.

47.   Cited in note 6 above.

48.   Hedrick realizes, correctly in my view, that specific meanings of parables arise (and vary) from the interplay of the story with the

historical circumstances and individual imaginations of the hearers and readers (59).

49. Hedrick notes that there are a few parables that deliberately use metaphor within the narrative (29, 32–33, 62). One should take care, however, to make sure that it is the internal force of the language of the narrative that deliberately evokes those referential horizons (as does the parable of the Leaven, 33) or whether it is the reader's imagination that "creates" these outside connections. Hedrick further argues that early Christians created these outside contacts by associating Jesus' parables, for the first time, with the kingdom of God. Early Christians made this attempt because they were trying to make sense out of these ordinary, occasional stories that were no longer directly relevant to their own situations.

50. Craig Blomberg, *Interpreting the Parables* (Downers Grove, IL: InterVarsity Press, 1990), 23. In my view, a more insightful critique of Jeremias's "laws of transformation," is found in Ivor H. Jones, *The Matthean Parables: A Literary and Historical Commentary* (Leiden: Brill, 1995), 56–89. For a vigorous critique of Blomberg, see Andrew Parker, *Painfully Clear,* 82–87. Parker contends that most of Jesus' parables are "attitude-straightening," where Jesus targeted people's "sick attitudes" to help restore them to "health" (68, 107).

51. Some scholars, given the weaknesses in form and redaction criticisms, have screeched to a halt in a methodological cul-de-sac and have despaired of determining the "authentic" voice of Jesus. Others have bypassed the arguments over precise historicity and have moved into purely literary approaches. Still others have pressed on, publishing red-letter editions of the parables (the Jesus Seminar) or looking for an "originating" structure (Bernard Brandon Scott). Blomberg chooses another, less-trodden path: He extends "authenticity" to all of the words attributed to Jesus in conjunction with the parables, including introductions, conclusions, and aphoristic generalizations (166). As C. M. Tuckett notes, "almost every account of every parable in all three gospels is taken as authentic.... [T]his looks very much like special pleading to press a theory just a bit too far." See Tuckett's review of Blomberg's book in *Biblica* 72:4 (1991) 582–85. Perhaps a quote from a "mainstream" scholar is appropriate: "There is every sign of a lengthy and complex history of tradition which extended through the oral, written, and redactional levels of development. One can at times easily discern stages in the growth of certain parables.... [But] the task of separating

the various layers seems to me far more complex than is often realized." Werner G. Kümmel, *Introduction to the New Testament,* trans. Howard Clark Kee (Nashville, TN: Abingdon, 1975), 536–37.

52. Blomberg's matrix seems to form a procrustean bed in which each parable is forced to fit. C. M. Tuckett also notes the "slightly bland and somewhat disappointing" interpretations and gently laments the lack of "deeper sensitivity." He also asserts that Blomberg's "agenda" causes him to miss out on vital exegetical decisions (583–84). Yet, other recent works reflect a similar concern for "propositional truth" in metaphor. See Edmund Arens, *Kommunikative Handlungen* (Düsseldorf: Patmos, 1982), who understands parables as rhetorical metaphors closely tied to particular contexts and that presuppose propositional truths. See also, Timothy A. Deibler, "A Philosophical Semantic Intentionality Theory of Metaphor" (Ph.D. Dissertation, Rice University, 1989). Deibler concludes: "There is no such thing as a special kind of truth over and above literal truth" (224, cf. 228–29). Charles Hedrick, in contrast, believes that any attempt to reduce the stories to a propositional meaning focuses not on the story but behind the story on the (hypothetical construct of the) mind of the inventor (*Parables as Poetic Fictions,* 57).

53. John W. Sider, *Interpreting the Parables: A Hermeneutical Guide to Their Meaning* (Grand Rapids, MI: Zondervan, 1995). This book collects and significantly expands the insights of various articles Sider had published over a number of years (beginning in 1981). Sider assumes the essential authenticity of the parables in the gospel texts: "...Jesus' parables are *embedded literary subsets* [emphasis his] of his discourse and the evangelists' narrative, and their meaning is subject to the control of Jesus' authoritative intent" (211). For a rebuttal of this position, see my arguments in chapter 3 above: When a parable is embedded in a larger narrative, the author's voice enters into a dialogue with the parable and reverberates with the original utterance of the creator of the parable.

54. Compare John Dominic Crossan's statement that "You can prove nothing by analogy," in his *In Parables* (New York: Harper & Row, 1973), 74–75. In addition, Sider only partially recognizes that the words "moral and social" should also include social and economic aspects (see 171–91).

55. The four exceptions to this rule are the "example stories" of the Good Samaritan, the Rich Fool, the Rich Man and Lazarus, and the

Pharisee and the Publican. This distinction, which has been in existence since Jülicher, has been challenged by such scholars as Funk, Breech, Crossan, and Scott, who argue that the stories were originally parables that should be understood metaphorically in relation with the kingdom of God. For a defense of the position that Jesus used these parables as example stories, see Wilhelm C. Linss, "Example Stories?" *Currents in Theology and Mission* 17 (1990) 447–53. For a defense of similes as "mere analogy" and their relationship to metaphors from a different perspective, see Teresa Bridgeman, "On the *Like*ness of Similes and Metaphors," *The Modern Language Review* 91:1 (1996) 65–79.

56. Andrew Parker, however, cautions against the overreliance on analogy: "[Y]ou can never sum up a parable by simply writing out its basic analogy because, even if you are satisfied that you have managed not to betray the parable's logic, you remain miles away from describing the full impact on the listener when he or she bridges the parable's gap and makes the connection. You always find that you want to throw such analogies away, for the parable accomplishes something no analogy can…" (*Painfully Clear,* 62–63).

57. As George Shillington similarly observed, "The narrative structure of Jesus' parables is not straight illustration; it is tinged with riddle" (*Jesus and His Parables,* 16–17).

58. As noted concerning epithets, metaphors, similes, and so forth, by Mikhail Bakhtin: "Author and Hero in Aesthetic Activity," in *Art and Answerability* (Austin: University of Texas Press, 1990), 46.

59. Mikhail Bakhtin, "Epic and Novel," in *The Dialogic Imagination: Four Essays* (Austin: University of Texas Press, 1981), 30–31.

60. For a philosophical explanation of why this is true for all historical events and the texts which attempt to portray them, see Mikhail Bakhtin, "The Problem of the Text in Linguistics, Philology, and the Human Sciences: An Experiment in Philosophical Analysis," in *Speech Genres and Other Essays* (Austin: University of Texas Press, 1986), especially. 108–9.

Conclusion

1. But Charles Hedrick and Craig Blomberg, although they arrive at very different conclusions in their own work on the parables,

have offered somewhat similar assessments of the current state of research. See Charles W. Hedrick, "Prolegomena to Reading Parables: Luke 13:6–9 As a Test Case," in *Review and Expositor* 94 (1997) 179–97; Craig L. Blomberg, "The Parables of Jesus: Current Trends and Needs in Research," in *Studying the Historical Jesus: Evaluations of Current Research,* ed. Bruce Chilton and Craig Evans (Leiden: Brill, 1994), 231–54.

2. Mikhail Bakhtin, a trained classicist, noted that "the most ancient forms for representing language were organized by laughter" (*The Dialogic Imagination,* 50). Laughter can be an important part of the active, engaging, and dialogic nature of *parable.* Parables thus, in Bakhtin's terminology, have some "carnivalizing" influences. Parallel albeit unconnected ideas can be found in works such as, for example, D. Wayne Sandifer, "The Humor of the Absurd in the Parables of Jesus," *1991 SBL Seminar Papers* (Atlanta: Scholars Press, 1991), 287–97, and George Aichele, Jr., "The Fantastic in the Parabolic Language of Jesus," *Neotestamentica* 24:1 (1990) 93–105.

3. The following is my "rejoinder," a simplistic version of my "Bakhtinian" perspective on the nature of the parables. It is culled from a number of Bakhtin's works.

For Further Reading

Bailey, Kenneth E. *Poet and Peasant: A Literary Approach to the Parables in Luke.* Grand Rapids, MI: Eerdmans, 1976; *Through Peasant Eyes.* Grand Rapids, MI: Eerdmans, 1980. An "Oriental exegesis" of the parables in Luke that combines standard tools of "Western scholarship" with cultural insights gained from ancient literature, contemporary peasants, and Syriac and Arabic versions of the New Testament.

Blomberg, Craig. *Interpreting the Parables.* Downers Grove, IL: InterVarsity Press, 1990. A conservative response to the application of historical-critical and literary approaches to the parables. Included is a defense of the authenticity of the sayings of Jesus and the presence of allegory in the "original" parables.

Boucher, Madeleine. *The Mysterious Parable: A Literary Study.* The Catholic Quarterly Monograph Series 6. Washington, DC: The Catholic Biblical Association of America, 1977; *The Parables.* Wilmington, DE: Michael Glazier, 1981. Contends that Jesus' parables are primarily rhetorical (constructed to persuade) not primarily poetic (created to be contemplated or enjoyed). Poetic elements are always subordinated to the parable's rhetorical function. The second volume provides a brief commentary on each parable in the Synoptic Gospels.

Breech, James. *The Silence of Jesus: The Authentic Voice of the Historical Man.* Philadelphia: Fortress Press, 1983. Seeks to recover the

139

"original Jesus" by perceiving parables as a window to Jesus' understanding of human existence. Like the works of Fyodor Dostoevsky and J. D. Salinger, Jesus' parables advocate a "hyperindividualism" that is committed to someone or something beyond one's self.

Carlston, Charles E. *The Parables of the Triple Tradition.* Philadelphia: Fortress Press, 1975. A redactional study of sixteen parables common to Mark, Matthew, and Luke.

Carter, Warren, and John Paul Heil. *Matthew's Parables: Audience-Oriented Perspectives.* The Catholic Biblical Quarterly Series 30. Washington, DC: The Catholic Biblical Association of America, 1998. Focuses on what happens as Matthew's audience interacts with the parables in their present form and in their current placement within the plot of Matthew's Gospel.

Crossan, John Dominic. *Cliffs of Fall: Paradox and Polyvalence in the Parables of Jesus.* New York: Seabury, 1980. Three essays that explore aspects of paradox and polyvalence in the parables of Jesus. For example, utilizing the work of Jacques Derrida, Crossan argues that all language is metaphoric; metaphor creates a void of meaning and a polyvalence that generate the "free play" of interpretations.

Crossan, John Dominic. *The Dark Interval. Towards a Theology of Story.* Niles, IL: Argus, 1975. Uses structuralist models to argue that Jesus' parables are world-shattering invitations to live without myth so that the kingdom of God may arrive.

Crossan, John Dominic. *Finding is the First Act. Trove Folktales and Jesus' Treasure Parable.* Philadelphia: Fortress, 1979. Compares the structure of the parable of the hidden treasure (Mt 13:44) with other Jewish treasure stories and the wider background of the entire tradition of other "treasure plots" in world folklore. Matthew 13:44 is seen as a "metaparable" that succeeds precisely to the extent it fails.

Crossan, John Dominic. *In Parables: The Challenge of the Historical Jesus.* New York: Harper & Row, 1973. Parables are poetic metaphors that portray a "permanent eschatology" through an advent of a radical new world of possibility, a reversal of ordinary expectations, and a call to action in response to the divine will.

Crossan, John Dominic. *Raid on the Articulate.* New York: Harper & Row, 1976. Compares the "comic eschatology" of Jesus' parables with works of Jorge Luis Borges. Crossan emphasizes play, polyvalence, and indeterminacy.

Culbertson, Philip L. *A Word Fitly Spoken.* Albany: SUNY Press, 1995. Argues that the parables of Jesus are Jewish "halakhic midrash," reinterpretations that draw out the inner meaning of (legal) texts.

Dodd, C. H. *The Parables of the Kingdom.* rev. ed. Glasgow: Collins, 1961. Makes extended use of form-critical methods to examine the "pre-literary" stages of the parables and offers a detailed interpretation of the teaching of Jesus as related to the actual circumstances of his ministry. The parables proclaim that the kingdom of God is realized in the life and teachings of Jesus.

Donahue, John R. *The Gospel as Parable.* Philadelphia: Fortress Press, 1988. Reviews previous works on parable, metaphor, and narrative and then studies parables primarily as texts within the literary and theological contexts of each gospel.

Drury, John. *The Parables in the Gospels: History and Allegory.* New York: Crossroads, 1985. Insists that interpreting the parables within their gospel contexts restores their power and sense of drama. He tries to establish the meaning and use of the parables that the authors of the gospels inherited from Jewish tradition and seeks to understand the parables in their gospel contexts.

Funk, Robert W. *Language, Hermeneutic, and the Word of God.* New York: Harper & Row, 1966. The chapter "The Parable as Metaphor" argues that metaphor is a bearer of the reality to which it refers and that the parables, as metaphors, are "open ended."

Funk, Robert W., Bernard Brandon Scott, and James R. Butts. Eds. *The Parables of Jesus.* Sonoma, CA: Polebridge Press, 1988. Results from the Jesus Seminar's deliberations on the authenticity of the parables of Jesus as found in the Synoptic Gospels. The parables are printed in red or pink to indicate "authentic" parables and in gray or black to indicate parables that Jesus probably did not create, in their view. The book includes a brief introduction to the work and methodology of the Jesus Seminar.

Hedrick, Charles. *Parables as Poetic Fictions: The Creative Voice of Jesus*. Peabody, MA: Hendrickson, 1994. The parables of Jesus are ordinary, freely invented, fictional stories that realistically portray aspects of first-century Palestinian life. Therefore an interpretation should not go outside the "world of the story" unless it is mandated by "particular semantic markers" in the story itself (which rarely happens).

Herzog, William R. *Parables as Subversive Speech*. Louisville, KY: W/JKP, 1994. Views Jesus' parables through the lens of the "pedagogy of the oppressed," which focuses on how oppression serves the interests of the ruling class. Parables are social analyses that explore how human beings could respond to break the spiral of violence and the cycle of poverty created by such exploitation.

Jeremias, Joachim. *The Parables of Jesus*. New York: Charles Scribner's Sons, 1972. Investigates the ways in which the original parables of Jesus were transformed by the early church and tries to recover those parables, their main themes, and their original contexts during the ministry of the historical Jesus.

Jeremias, Joachim. *Rediscovering the Parables*. New York: Charles Scribner's Sons, 1966. A revision of his *The Parables of Jesus* for a wider circle of readers by omitting that book's "purely technical and linguistic content."

Jones, Ivor H. *The Matthean Parables: A Literary and Historical Commentary*. Leiden: Brill, 1995. Investigates how the parables in Matthew can shed light on the structure, purpose, and genre of the gospel as a whole. Brings together many of the insights of recent scholarship to study the parables in Matthew. The "emblematic" language of the parables opens the paths for others to respond in their own ways. Jones also includes detailed studies of the individual Matthean parables.

Jülicher, Adolph. *Die Gleichnisreden Jesu.* Darmstadt: Wissenschaftliche Buchgesellschaft, 1969. Originally published in 1886 and never translated into English, this work inaugurated the modern study of parables. Parables are similes, not metaphors, and the early church and the gospel authors obscured the message of the historical Jesus with layers of allegory, descriptive supplementation, and interpretive application.

Kingsbury, Jack Dean. *The Parables of Jesus in Matthew 13.* London: SPCK, 1969. A redactional study of the parables in Matthew 13 that contends that the author redacted the parables to meet the situation of his church and its disputes with Pharisaic Judaism in particular.

Kissinger, Warren. *The Parables of Jesus: A History of Interpretation and Bibliography.* Metuchen, NJ: Scarecrow Press, 1979. Includes a history of interpretation of the parables from Irenaeus through John Dominic Crossan (through 1976) and a bibliography of works on the parables (through 1977).

Klauck, Hans-Josef. *Allegorie und Allegorese in synoptischen Gleichnistexten.* Munster: Aschendorff, 1978. Reviews research on allegory since Jülicher and discusses allegory in ancient literature and modern criticism. He analyzes specific gospel passages and concludes that allegory must be distinguished from allegorism and allegorizing and that allegorical elements are part of the authentic parables of Jesus.

Linnemann, Eta. *The Jesus of the Parables: Introduction and Exposition.* London: SPCK, 1966. Jesus' parables are "language events" that compel listeners to make a decision.

McArthur, Harvey K., and Robert M. Johnston. *They Also Taught in Parables.* Grand Rapids, MI: Zondervan, 1990. Presents translations of

115 tannaitic parables (i.e., before 220 C.E.). Also includes a wide range of aspects concerning rabbinic parables.

McFague, Sallie. *Speaking in Parables*. Philadelphia: Fortress Press, 1975. Parable is an extended metaphor in which meaning is found only within the story itself although it is not exhausted by the story. The meaning is "nontransferable," and the metaphor shocks us into a new awareness. Parables become models of theological reflection.

Noël, Timothy. "Parables in Context: Developing a Narrative-Critical Approach to Parables in Luke," Ph.D. dissertation. Louisville, KY: The Southern Baptist Theological Seminary, 1986. Contains a helpful summary of parable research and is one of the first works to apply literary-critical methods to parables in Luke.

Parker, Andrew. *Painfully Clear: The Parables of Jesus*. Sheffield: Sheffield Academic Press, 1996. Contends that the great majority of Jesus' parables were "attitude-straightening"; they were meant to be "painfully clear" because most were intended for people with sick attitudes and were designed to make them aware of their condition and to restore them to health.

Perrin, Norman. *Jesus and the Language of the Kingdom*. Philadelphia: Fortress Press, 1976. The kingdom of God is the ultimate referent of all Jesus' parables, but it is a symbol that can represent or evoke a whole range or series of conceptions. As a symbol, it has deep roots in Jewish self-identity as the people of God, and Jesus' parables mediated to the hearer an experience of the kingdom. Also includes a helpful review of the parable scholarship of his contemporaries.

Scott, Bernard Brandon. *Hear Then the Parable: A Commentary on the Parables of Jesus*. Minneapolis: Fortress Press, 1989. Defines *parable* as a Jewish *mashal* that employs a short narrative fiction to reference a symbol. Accents the literary, linguistic, and metaphorical elements of the parables with an emphasis on the relation of the parables with the mythological kingdom of God. The commentary section analyzes each parable of Jesus in the present literary context of each gospel, in its prior development in the oral tradition, and in the "originating structure" within the ministry of the historical Jesus.

Scott, Bernard Brandon. *Jesus, Symbol-Maker for the Kingdom.* Philadelphia: Fortress Press, 1981. Argues that structuralist models developed in parable criticism provide a basis to construct a coherent insight into the historical Jesus' language as a whole.

Shillington, V. George. Ed. *Jesus and His Parables.* Edinburgh: T & T Clark, 1997. A collection of ten essays on the parables of Jesus from differing scholars and perspectives. Attempts to offer fresh glimpses into the life and vision of the historical figure of Jesus.

Sider, John W. *Interpreting the Parables: A Hermeneutical Guide to Their Meaning.* Grand Rapids, MI: Zondervan, 1995. Argues that a *parable* is a "discursive or narrative analogy in the service of a moral or spiritual argument." Almost all of Jesus' parables convey meaning by elaborating one proportional analogy, often multiplied into several analogies, which results in parable becoming allegory.

Stern, David. *Parables and Midrash.* Cambridge, MA: Harvard University Press, 1991. Investigates the Jewish *mashal* and seeks to offer a full description that includes aspects such as composition and exegetical techniques, rhetoric, poetics, and place in the history of Hebrew literature. The *mashal* is "an illusive narrative told for an ulterior purpose" whose purpose can usually be defined as praise or blame of a specific situation of the author and audience of this fictional narrative. As such, the *mashal* actively elicits from its audience the application of its message.

Thoma, Clemens, and Michael Wyschogrod. Eds. *Parable and Story in Judaism and Christianity.* Mahwah, NJ: Paulist Press, 1989. A collection of essays from various scholars about parables and other stories as found in Jewish and Christian literature.

Tolbert, Mary Ann. *Perspectives on the Parables*. Philadelphia: Fortress Press, 1979. Seeks to preserve the integrity of the parables and of contemporary experiences of them. Includes guidelines for interpretation and a discussion of the problem of multiple interpretations and the openness of parables. The structure of a parable does not generate "a meaning," but it provides basic constraints and possibilities within which a variety of meanings may be perceived.

Via, Dan Otto. *The Parables: Their Literary and Existential Dimension*. Philadelphia: Fortress Press, 1967. Investigates the parables as "aesthetic objects," carefully organized, self-contained ("autonomous"), coherent literary compositions. Thus Via argues that we can analyze the understanding of human existence inherent in their literary form and content with virtually no reference to their original historical context.

Westermann, Claus. *The Parables of Jesus in Light of the Old Testament*. Minneapolis: Fortress Press, 1990. Discusses the use of parable, simile, metaphor, and allegory in sections of the Hebrew Bible. They are not merely illustrative but are part of the wider contexts in which they belong. Comparisons are an essential element of what the Hebrew Bible says about God and God's relationship with human beings. The parables of the gospels possess the same general characteristics and must be interpreted as a central aspect of Jesus' pressing message about the approaching kingdom of God.

Wilder, Amos. *The Language of the Gospel*. Rev. Ed. New York: Harper & Row, 1971. The eighteen-page chapter on Jesus' parables established the parameters for discussions for years to come. Jesus used these images to mediate reality and life, and his metaphors impart an image with a certain shock to the imagination that directly conveys a vision of what is signified. The hearer not only participates in this reality but is "invaded" by it.

Young, Brad H. *Jesus and his Jewish Parables.* New York: Paulist Press, 1989. Contends that parables must be studied as a unique genre of teaching that is preserved only in rabbinic literature and the gospels. Also argues that "kingdom of heaven" refers to God's reign as a present reality among those persons who accept the call to obey the divine will.

Scripture Index

Hebrew Bible

Nm

23:7	43
23:18	43
24:3	43
24:15	43
24:20	43
24:21	43
24:23	43

Dt

4:30	49
28:37	43

Jgs

9:7–15	44

1 Sm

10:12	42, 117
24:13	42, 117

2 Sm

12:1–4	45, 55

1 Kgs

9:7	43

2 Kgs

14:9	45

Jb

29	43

Ps

49	43
78	43

Prv

1:6	43
9:1–6	44
9:13–18	44

Is

5:1–6	45
14:4–23	43
28:23–29	44

Jer			*24:43–44*	90
3:12	51		25:1–13	90
3:25	51		25:14–30	6
24:9	43		25:15–30	105
31:9	51			
			Mk	
Ezk			4	64, 108
14:8	43		4:1–9	5, 89
15:1–8	44		4:1–34	63, 123
16:1–54	44		4:10–12	11
17:3–10	43, 45		4:11–12	56
19:2–9	44		4:25	6
19:10–14	44		4:26–29	86
23:1–9	44		4:33	117
24:3–5	43		7:15–17	117
24:3–14	44			
			Lk	
Micah			4:23	43, 117
2:4	43		7:31–34	4
			8:4–8	5
			8:9–10	12
			10:25–27	26
New Testament			10:25–29	70
			10:25–37	36
Mt			10:29	109
9:37–38	52		10:30–37	5, 104
10:1–8	10		10:36	70, 109
11:16–19	4		12:5–21	117
13	10–11, 80, 106, 108, 143		12:13–21	60
13:1–9	5		12:35–40	75
13:10–17	11, 12		12:39–40	90
13:24–30	76, 89		14:1–14	64
13:33	117		14:7–11	117
13:44	29, 31, 140		14:7–24	64
13:45	29		14:16–24	64
18:32–33	60		15	81
20:1–16	71, 72			
20:13–15	60			

15:3	37
15:11–32	98
16:1–9	74
16:19–31	60, 61
18:1	60
18:18–23	36
19:11	105
19:11–27	74
19:12–27	6

Apocrypha or Pseudepigrapha

Gospel of Thomas
81:28—82:3	29

Sir
39:2	43

1 Enoch
37–71	45

Other Books in This Series

What are they saying about the Prophets?
  by David P. Reid, SS. CC.
What are they saying about Moral Norms?
  by Richard M. Gula, S.S.
What are they saying about Sexual Morality?
  by James P. Hanigan
What are they saying about Dogma?
  by William E. Reiser, S.J.
What are they saying about Peace and War?
  by Thomas A. Shannon
What are they saying about Papal Primacy?
  by J. Michael Miller, C.S.B.
What are they saying about Matthew?
  by Donald Senior, C.P.
What are they saying about Matthew's Sermon on the Mount?
  by Warren Carter
What are they saying about Biblical Archaeology?
  by Leslie J. Hoppe. O.F.M.
What are they saying about Theological Method?
  by J.J. Mueller, S.J.
What are they saying about Virtue?
  by Anthony J. Tambasco
What are they saying about Genetic Engineering?
  by Thomas A. Shannon
What are they saying about Salvation?
  by Rev. Denis Edwards
What are they saying about Mark?
  by Frank J. Matera
What are they saying about Luke?
  by Mark Allan Powell
What are they saying about John?
  by Gerard S. Sloyan
What are they saying about Acts?
  by Mark Allan Powell

Other Books in This Series

What are they saying about the Ministerial Priesthood?
by Rev. Daniel Donovan

What are they saying about the Social Setting
of the New Testament?
by Carolyn Osiek

What are they saying about Scripture and Ethics?
(Revised and Expanded Ed.)
by William C. Spohn

What are they saying about Unbelief?
by Michael Paul Gallagher, S.J.

What are they saying about Masculine Spirituality?
by David James

What are they saying about Environmental Ethics?
by Pamela Smith

What are they saying about the Formation of Pauline Churches?
by Richard S. Ascough

What are they saying about the Trinity?
by Anne Hunt

What are they saying about the Formation of Israel?
by John J. McDermott